Esoteric Orders
and Their Work

Other books by Dion Fortune

Occult Study
Machinery of the Mind
The Esoteric Philosophy of Love and Marriage
Psychology of the Servant Problem
The Soya Bean
Esoteric Orders and Their Work
The Problem of Purity
Sane Occultism (to publish as *What is Occultism?* Weiser, 2001)
Training and Work of an Initiate
Mystical Meditations on the Collects
Spiritualism in the Light of Occult Science
Psychic Self-Defense
Through the Gates of Death
Glastonbury—Avalon of the Heart
The Mystical Qabalah
Practical Occultism in Daily Life
Applied Magic
Aspects of Occultism
The Magical Battle of Britain

Occult Fiction
The Demon Lover
The Goat-Foot God
Moon Magic
The Sea Priestess
The Secrets of Dr. Taverner
The Winged Bull

Esoteric Orders
and Their Work

DION FORTUNE

Foreword by Gareth Knight

SAMUEL WEISER, INC.

York Beach, Maine

First published in 2000 by
Samuel Weiser, Inc.
P. O. Box 612
York Beach, ME 03910-0612
www.weiserbooks.com

07 06 05 04 03 02 01 00
10 9 8 7 6 5 4 3 2 1

Library of Congress Cataloging-in-Publication Data

Fortune, Dion.
    Esoteric orders and their work / Dion Fortune.
       p. cm.
    Originally published: London: Rider & Co., 1928.
  With new foreword by Gareth Knight.
    Includes index.
    ISBN 1-57863-184-X (alk. paper)
    1. Occultism. I. Title.
  BF1411 .F564 2000
  135—dc21   00-040892

Printed in the United States of America
BJ

The paper used in this publication meets the minimum requirements of the
American National Standard for Information Sciences—Permanence of
Paper for Printed Library Materials Z39.48-1992(R1997).

CONTENTS

FOREWORD
by Gareth Knight

FIRST published in 1928, *The Esoteric Orders and Their Work,* along with its companion volume, *The Training and Work of an Initiate* (1930), represented the first serious statement of Dion Fortune's aims and ideals in launching her famous school, the Fraternity of the Inner Light.

Her Fraternity was to be nothing less than an Esoteric Order consisting of trained Initiates. *The Esoteric Orders and Their Work* thus expressed her vision of what such groups should do, and *The Training and Work of an Initiate* declared how its members should be trained to fulfill this group purpose.

At this time Dion Fortune had reached the midpoint of her occult career. This began in 1916, when she met her first teacher, Dr. Theodore Moriarty, who so impressed her with his powers that she threw up her work as a therapist at the Medico-Psychological Clinic, convinced that an orthodox approach to the mysteries of the human mind now seemed completely inadequate.

She later wrote about the occult circumstances of this first meeting with Moriarty as a short story, in "Blood Lust," the first in a series titled *The Secrets of Dr. Taverner.*

In the early years of her occult career, she imbibed most of the popular teachings of the Theosophical Society, and Annie Besant's *The Ancient Wisdom* had a profound effect upon her, inducing the vision of a contact with two powerful spiritual beings somewhere in the

Himalayas. For her practical training, however, she turned not to the esoteric section of the Theosophical Society, but to Theodore Moriarty, who taught a system of what he called Universal Theosophy, imparting a Western slant to Blavatsky's predominantly Eastern-based philosophy. He was also a man of considerable charisma and power to judge from Dion Fortune's memoirs of him in *Psychic Self-Defense*.

Moriarty was an advocate of co-masonry, that is to say, masonic ritual and initiation open to women, and by 1919 had founded a temple in London for its practice. From the rolls that survive, it would appear that, apart from himself, the lodge was composed entirely of women. Whether this was from policy, by chance, or through natural affinity is open to conjecture. Certainly, from later remarks she made, Dion Fortune was not much enthused by her experience with esoteric groups consisting only of women, and advocated a balanced representation of the sexes wherever possible.

While she had great admiration and respect for Moriarty, it would seem that the work of his group did not entirely satisfy her, for in 1919 she became an initiate of the Alpha et Omega Temple of what had originally been known as the Hermetic Order of the Golden Dawn. This Temple was under the aegis of the Scottish novelist J. W. Brodie Innes, and had two lodges, one in Edinburgh and one in London. Dion Fortune joined the latter under the immediate tutelage of an adept who also happened to be an old family friend, Maiya Curtis-Webb (later Tranchell-Hayes).

She was at this time still known as Violet Mary Firth, and her pen name—Dion Fortune—derives from her magical name within the Temple, where she was known as Soror Deo Non Fortuna. She was plainly no ordinary esoteric student, and although she may not have shone too much in performing the minutiae of the Order meditation discipline, she gave every sign of being capable of developing her own inner contacts. These talents went beyond the abilities of most other initiates, and also beyond the scope of most spiritualist mediums.

During 1921 she experimented along these lines under Maiya Curtis-Webb's supervision, and by the Autumnal Equinox of the same year had developed so far as to be working publicly with Frederick Bligh Bond at Glastonbury.

Bligh Bond is best known for his archaeological work upon the ruins of Glastonbury Abbey, with which he had been associated since 1907. He made some remarkable discoveries which, it turned out, were the result of following instructions obtained through a clairvoyant by automatic writing. He did not admit to this source of revelation until the publication of his book, *The Gate of Remembrance* in 1918—whereupon the scandalised church authorities, who now owned the ruins, took firm steps to marginalise him from any more work on the site. Working alongside him in 1921, Dion Fortune picked up on an inner group very close to his heart and mind, who were known as the Watchers of Avalon.

However, their collaboration did not last long. Bligh Bond, beset by various difficulties including domestic ones, sought a more congenial intellectual climate in America, and he moved there in 1924.

Dion Fortune stayed on in Glastonbury, and in 1922 she met up with Charles Thomas Loveday, a Royal Flying Corps veteran, who had a love of music, an enthusiasm for the new science of radio and powerful Harley Davidson motorcycles! Some fifteen years her senior, Loveday was to become her lifetime friend, and moral and financial supporter, in an avuncular rather than a romantic liaison. Their meeting was entirely coincidental, as casual visitors one moonlit night at Chalice Well, a residential hostel run by Alice Buckton at the foot of the Tor. Their instant recognition of a common destiny sparked the foundation of a small group of like-minded friends that eventually developed into the Fraternity of the Inner Light.

During 1923, with Loveday as her diligent scribe, Dion Fortune began to make contacts with the Masters, or Inner Plane Adepti as her school preferred to call them. These contacts were to guide and instruct her in everything that followed throughout the rest of her life.

The communications began with a wide variety of teachings, the more elementary of which were published as *The Esoteric Philosophy of Love and Marriage,* while the more advanced were eventually released to the public as *The Cosmic Doctrine.* Of lasting practical importance was their acquisition of two pieces of real estate in 1924. One was a site upon which to build a chalet at the foot of Glastonbury Tor, opposite Chalice Well, and the other a house in the west end of London to develop as administrative headquarters with both lodge and lecture room facilities.

They required a few more years to find their permanent identity as a Fraternity in 1927, and the period of preparation was a far from easy one. Their first external corporate identity was as The Christian Mystic Lodge of the Theosophical Society. This small group had been founded in 1919, and for the first six years of its existence followed a fairly quiet existence as a kind of halfhouse between Theosophy and Christianity. All this was to change when, on instructions from her inner contacts, Dion Fortune, Charles Loveday and their friends joined it in 1925, and soon after Dion Fortune became its President.

In this role they placed themselves within the Theosophical Society in direct conflict with another movement within it that, under the aegis of Annie Besant and C. W. Leadbeater, had been gaining ground since 1909. This was the Star in the East movement which sought to promote the young Krishnamurti as a spiritual world leader, virtually ranking as a second coming of the Christ. This caused considerable controversy in various esoteric circles, including the Theosophical Society itself, and other major occultists, such as Rudolf Steiner also had grave reservations about it. Dion Fortune's contacts appeared very concerned on account of it being what they considered to be an oriental interpretation distorting the true religious heritage of the West.

Although they had been instructed to try to avoid a deliberate confrontation, considerable heat was generated at the time, and by the end of 1927, Dion Fortune and her friends had broken free to form their own independent organisation, the Community (later Fraternity) of the Inner Light. The Star in the East movement came to an end in 1929, with Krishnamurti's own repudiation of it.

In 1927 things also came to a head with Mina MacGregor Mathers who, not without reason, felt that this young member of her Temple was really too much of an independent spirit. The events at the Vernal Equinox this year, which Dion Fortune later wrote about in *Psychic Self-Defense,* brought an end to her formal affiliation to the Golden Dawn tradition, at least for the time being. Such links were to be made and broken twice more in her life, first with Hope Hughes of the Hermes Temple of the Stella Matutina in 1930, and then with Maiya Tranchell-Hayes again in 1940.

In October 1927, the Fraternity of the Inner Light proclaimed its presence with the first issue of *The Inner Light Magazine* as a valid Esoteric Order in its own right, with its own inner contacts and training system for initiates. The following year saw publication of *The Esoteric Orders and Their Work,* to be followed in 1930 by its companion volume, *The Training and Work of an Initiate.*

In another respect, 1927 was a crucial year in that Dion Fortune married Dr. Thomas Penry Evans. He was a Welshman of humble origins who enlisted as a private soldier in the Artists Rifles at the beginning of the 1914-1918 war and came out as a 2nd lieutenant in the Machine Gun Corps, when he somehow found the money and influence to enter medical school. He had been a lodger at Dion Fortune's London headquarters since 1925, along with his sister Hazel, a nurse who later married the first Director of Studies of the Fraternity. Early ambitions at this time included forming a group that also had a clinical function in esoteric healing, somewhat along the lines of the Dr. Taverner ideal. This vision foundered, it would appear, through the conflict between the demands of a normal medical career on Penry Evans and that of playing a leading role in a burgeoning esoteric society.

In 1938 they went their separate ways. He via the Spanish Civil War, as an advisor on child nutrition to the Republican government. When he returned it was not to Dion Fortune or the Society of the Inner Light. They were formally divorced in 1945, and after her death, he remarried and ended his days in 1959 as a popular and respected country doctor.

However, during the 1930s the Fraternity they jointly headed up, along with C. T. Loveday, developed with increasing success. After Mina MacGregor Mathers's death in 1928, affiliation to the Golden Dawn tradition was renewed in 1930 via the Hermes Temple of the Stella Matutina in Bristol. This, however, was not destined to outlast the coming and going of Israel Regardie, who after initiation into the Hermes Temple roundly condemned its running, and from 1937 proceeded to publish its papers. As Dion Fortune had openly supported Regardie during his time in Britain, and shared his belief in getting rid of unnecessary secrecy, she also found herself *persona non grata* with her erstwhile friend Hope Hughes, head of the Hermes Temple.

Oddly enough, that was not the end of her Golden Dawn association, for in 1940 she teamed up again with her former teacher, Maiya Tranchell-Hayes. They worked together for at least two years, one consequence of which was a body of teaching based on the Arthurian legend— most of it subsequently incorporated into Gareth Knight's *The Secret Tradition in Arthurian Legend.*

The 1930s brought about a remarkable development, not only in the Fraternity of the Inner Light, but in Dion Fortune herself. One undoubtedly sparked off the other, for most of her subsequent books first appeared as series articles in *The Inner Light Magazine.* This included her major work, *The Mystical Qabalah,* which was eventually published in volume form in 1935, and has served as a medium of instruction for Inner Light students and initiates ever since.

She also sought to add flesh and bones to Qabalistic philosophy in a series of instructive esoteric novels that include *The Goat-Foot God, The Winged Bull, The Sea Priestess,* and *Moon Magic.* This led in turn to a number of semi-public Rites of Pan and of Isis, performed at a converted church called the Belfry, which might be regarded as a forerunner, in some respects, to the latter day fashion for "workshops" yet which also, in a strange way, recapitulated what S. L. and Mina MacGregor Mathers had done a generation before in Paris.

The Fraternity also began to have a high profile presence on the esoteric and literary scene. In conjunction with the popular academic Bernard Bromage, she hosted a number of public discussions on occultism in literature, with guests that included leading figures of literary London at that time. These included Christina Foyle of the famous bookshop, and novelists such as Marjorie Bowen, Claude Houghton, and Bertha Ruck, and well-known writers on psychical research, such as Elliott O'Donnell.

The outbreak of war put a stop to all this, but undeterred by the blitz or problems of travel and holding meetings, Dion Fortune kept in touch with all her members, associates, and sympathisers with a series of Weekly Letters allied to a postal meditation group. The proceedings of these meetings have since been published in abridged form as Dion Fortune's *Magical Battle of Britain*. In 1941and 1942, the tide of war turned toward likely victory and she re-established the training of students while at the same time maintaining an energetic but ultimately abortive campaign to form a united front of spiritualism and occultism in preparation for the postwar years. None of this prevented her from pursuing more private advanced work in collaboration with her Deputy Warden W. K. Creasy and Maiya Tranchell-Hayes, including a restimulation of work on esoteric medicine by co-opting selected qualified medical practitioners into private meetings of senior members of the Fraternity.

The idea that has been subsequently put about that at this time she had become a spent force is based upon nothing but conjecture spiced with malicious gossip. She was very much a source of esoteric dynamism right up to her unexpected death from leukemia in January 1946.

At the time *The Esoteric Orders and Their Work* was first published, all this was in the future. Within its pages we find the relatively young 38-year-old head of a newly founded esoteric fraternity seeking to define her position, including where she has come from and where she hopes to be going.

Some of these origins are easy to identify from the opening chapters, which are more or less a synopsis, and a very lucid one, of the mainstream tradition of esoteric teaching that is to be found in Madame Blavatsky and her popularisers. There is also the emphasis upon an indigenous Western tradition, which she holds in common with Rudolf Steiner and his school, together with the threads of Masonic and Rosicrucian lines of thought and practice culled from the Golden Dawn teachings.

Thus we find, succinctly put, the occult traditions of ancient Root Races and guides of humanity through the ages, and of the influence in universal memory of the lost continent of Atlantis. This myth enjoys perennial popularity, despite all apparent geological evidence to the contrary, for it provides an "imaginal" history that in effective terms has every bit as much authenticity as "real" science-based pre-history. In its more remote universal and cosmic aspects, it also provides a system of callisthenics for the intuitive powers of the mind that can lead to higher consciousness.

In the midst of this, Dion Fortune makes certain assumptions that, although commonly accepted in her day, might now be quietly dropped. Of these we might mention the preoccupation with occult secrecy, which was almost an obsession with occultists of an older generation. There seems little justification for the belief that occult techniques must be kept secret on account of the uncontrollable powers that might be placed in the hands of the unworthy. Nowadays much of the practical side of occultism is freely dispensed in weekend workshops, although it has to be said that there are certain levels that are not appropriate for public display on account of unbalancing the emotional stability of the vulnerable and inexperienced (who may well be the last to regard themselves as such). This is a matter for discretion and discrimination within the current circumstances rather than a justification for a blanket ban on all practical instruction.

Much misinformation also exists about "words of power" which are popularly thought to require pronunciation only in a certain way. Most are unpronounceable anyway to anyone who is not a native of the linguistic tradition being used, while, as Israel Regardie has also pointed out, a lot may also depend upon different dialects and spellings.

All in all, the importance of an Esoteric Order rests on much the same criteria as a teaching establishment for any discipline, from playing the banjo to differential calculus. The better the tuition the easier and better the learning—and self-tuition can be a very poor substitute, particularly in matters like ritual, where practice in teamwork is needed.

Of course nothing is worse than an inadequate teacher. Esoteric schools have their rise and fall, like other institutions of learning. As Dion Fortune writes within these pages: "A great occultist will make a great occult school, but upon his death the mantle may fall upon unworthy shoulders and the glory be departed or turned to corruption" (see page 69).

Such remarks were given point by her observation of various temples of the former Golden Dawn. Some sought to blame Israel Regardie for much of this decline, but there is considerable point to his view that the Temples seemed doomed anyway by their false élitism, rigid secrecy, and lack of practical abilities. However, he lived to see a resurgence and revival of the Golden Dawn tradition in a later generation, in part instigated by himself.

No organisation is immune from its ups and downs, although in esoteric matters external observation can be a treacherous guide for there is often a very subjective projection from the eye of the beholder. The final judgment on all such things rests with a higher court, but the ability to survive from one generation to another is no bad indicator. In this respect, Dion Fortune's Fraternity gives evidence of health as it still exists, a lifetime and more after she founded it.

As to the future, that must depend upon the present, and whether you, who read these pages from Dion Fortune, find the inspiration of their call fans a flame of response within you.

INTRODUCTION

In all ages and among all races there has existed a tradition concerning certain esoteric schools or fraternities, wherein a secret wisdom unknown to the generality of mankind might be learnt, and to which admission was obtained by means of an initiation in which tests and ritual played their part. Whoever is familiar with the literature of folklore and anthropology knows that this belief exists among primitive peoples, from the Eskimos of the Arctic Circle to the Digger Indians of Tierra del Fuego. Whoever has also studied history knows that it has prevailed from the first dawn of human culture. To-day, in the centres of the civilised world, this belief is still alive ; and although it may be ridiculed by the orthodox-minded, an unprejudiced observer cannot fail to note that some of the noblest of men have been among its advocates, and that the greatest creative intelligences have, almost without exception, borne witness to a source of inspiration in the Unseen.

It is hard to believe that this rumour should be so widespread and so long-lived if it were entirely without foundation ; moreover, the fact that it has the same form among races who have had no intercourse with each other, such as the primitive Mexican and primitive Egyptian, is a further evidence in favour of its truth. It is not possible to demonstrate to those who are without the pale the existence of the organisations to which we have referred, because with the revelations of their secrets comes the obligation of silence. It is permissible, however, to give sufficient information to enable the earnest seeker to discern the path whereby he may approach the entrance to one or another of these schools, and for that purpose the following teaching concerning the esoteric orders and their functions is placed before the reader, though the proofs of the statements therein contained must of necessity be withheld until he shall have entitled himself to receive them.

The different occult schools declare themselves to be the holders of a secret traditional science, communicated to them, in the first place, by divine founders, and enriched and revised from time to time by great teachers; this science concerns the study of the causes that lie behind observable phenomena and condition them. After preliminary tests as to character and fitness, the occult fraternities are prepared to communicate the theory of this science to accepted candidates, and subsequently to convey the powers for its practical use by means of ritual initiations. These, briefly, are the claims made for the occult schools by those competent to speak on their behalf.

It is very frequently, and very reasonably, asked why it is that societies avowedly formed for the service of humanity, and having such valuable teaching to give, should not freely communicate it to all comers; should not, moreover, conduct active propaganda work in order to induce people to come and share in their wisdom, and not, as they appear to be doing, hide themselves away as if seeking by every possible device to avoid observation and prevent themselves being discovered by those who would learn from them.

The answer to this question will be found when the nature of occult science is understood. It concerns certain little-known powers of the human mind and certain little-understood aspects of nature. Were its researches into these subjects purely theoretical there would be no need to guard their findings so carefully, but the knowledge of the facts thus discovered immediately reveals their practical applications ; knowledge bestows power in this field of research, even more than in the fields explored by orthodox science, for the power thus rendered available is the power of the mind, and the effects of the use of this power are so far-reaching, whether for good or for evil, that it is a thing not lightly to be trusted into the hands of any human being. Just as the Dangerous Drugs Acts restrict the purchase and administration of potent drugs, so do those who are the custodians of this ancient traditional knowledge seek to safeguard its use. Being of so subtle a nature, it is impossible to guard it from abuse at the hands of the unscrupulous, and therefore its custodians do all in their power to prevent such persons from gaining access to it. Hence the restrictions with which its teaching is hedged about. But the restrictions are no more severe than those which attend the practice of medicine, for which a five years' onerous apprenticeship is required. We are so accustomed, however, to see spiritual teaching freely given, to hear the call, " Ho, every one that thirsteth, come ye to the waters of life and drink freely," that we cannot understand a policy which refuses any stream from this spring to those who are athirst.

The reason lies in the fact, which cannot be too clearly understood by its would-be neophytes, that occult science is a mental, not a spiritual, thing, and is neither good nor bad in itself, but only as it is used. It is potent for good or for evil; it can save souls which no other means could approach, and it can, even without evil intention, destroy them. It is no child's play, and few there be who are suited to that path to the heights. Nevertheless, for such as can adventure it, here is a noble quest for the soul, a true crusade against the Powers of Darkness and spiritual wickedness in high places. In the hidden places of the world there is so much occult evil, little suspected by those who have not met it face to face, that men and women of courage, strength, and the necessary knowledge are needed to deal with it.

The training given in occult schools is designed to produce the adept, a human being who, by intensive training, has raised himself or herself beyond the average development of humanity, and is dedicated to the service of God. Certain work in connection with evolution and the spiritual development and safeguarding of the nations is undertaken by highly-trained men and women, though their work is never seen and the place of their training is never known. Their actual training, it may be said, is given on the Inner Planes, and only the preliminary training which fits them for the Inner Schools takes place on the physical planes. Consciousness is prepared for its Great Quest, and adventures alone into the Unseen.

Not much can be told concerning this training, and not many are suitable for it, but enough has been said to give food for thought.

" The Esoteric Orders and their Work "

CHAPTER I

ESOTERICISM, OCCULTISM AND MYSTICISM

BEFORE embarking upon the study of the subject of this book, The Esoteric Orders and their Work, it is necessary to define the sense in which the term esotericism is used to include all aspects of super-physical science. To do this is a matter of some difficulty, as it is a relative term, being used in contra-distinction to exotericism. Esotericism begins where exotericism ends ; and as the boundaries of exoteric science are always advancing, so the boundaries of esotericism are always receding ; that which was taught to the initiates of Egypt is taught to the school-children of England. Reading, writing and arithmetic were once occult arts. So also are the profounder aspects of hypnosis, though some of its minor aspects have been rediscovered by exoteric scientists. As evolution advances, the average man becomes capable of that which once was only possible to the exceptional man. As the civilised man is to the savage, so is the adept to the average man. The powers of the civilised man appear miraculous to the savage because he does not know the laws to which they conform ; but the civilised man knows only too well that he does not transcend the realm of law when he flies like a bird or heals the sick ; he achieves his results by knowing certain natural laws and utilising them, and so does the adept.

The individual savage may be capable of benefiting by education, or he may not ; it depends upon his capacity. The average man may be capable of benefiting by initiation, or he may not ; it also depends upon his capacity ; but each individual should have the opportunity of advancing to the highest development of which he is capable. A certain degree of evolution must be reached before initiation becomes operative ; a student does not enter upon a post-graduate course until he has graduated. It is the function of exoteric religion to see to it that each member of the race reaches the normal standard of evolution ; it has to seek the lost sheep and raise the submerged tenth. Until a man has learnt the lessons of his faith he is not ready for the lessons of initiation. It is the function of the Lesser Mysteries to enable each individual admitted to their teaching to attain the highest degree of development of which he is capable. In the Lesser Mysteries are unfolded the latent capacities of man ; but in the Greater Mysteries are unfolded the hidden capacities of nature. The Lesser Mysteries deal with the subjective sphere, the Greater Mysteries with the objective sphere, and the one is the essential preliminary to the other. It is not possible for a man to command the elemental essences of nature unless he is master of the elemental aspects of his own nature, for the powers within, if rebellious, will betray him to the powers without. Discipline must precede dominion. We operate upon that which is without by the corresponding aspect that is within. If the nature be not purified, it will make a mixed contact when it touches the Unseen. The operations of occultism are based upon the powers of the will and the imagination; both blind forces. Unless they are controlled and directed by a motive which has relation to the universe as a whole, no ultimate synthesis is possible. The personality must be universalised by the ideal at which it aims in order that it may function as an organised part of the cosmic whole. It is this urge towards universalisation which is the ultimate hunger of the soul; the lesser self seeks to achieve it by drawing all things into itself in a rage of possession; the greater self seeks to achieve it by transcending the bounds of self and becoming one with the universe. There are two unions to be achieved : the self may become one with the universe by means of universal sympathy—this is the goal of the occultist; the self may also be made one with the Creator of the universe by means of absolute devotion—this is the goal of the mystic. But the occultist, having achieved his own goal, has not yet made the ultimate integration, he has not yet passed from the manifested phenomenal aspect into the cosmic; and the mystic, having achieved his transcendent union, cannot hold it, but must lapse back into the phenomenal universe. The ultimate integration can only be achieved by means of universal sympathy and absolute devotion united in one nature. Into such an one all things are gathered by means of sympathy, and he is in his turn gathered into the All by means of devotion.

This is the ultimate aim of evolution for the manifested universe as a whole; and he who goes by the Way of Initiation does but anticipate

evolution.   It is the function of the Mysteries to assist
the initiate to tread that section of the Path which
has already been explored, but beyond lies a section
that is known to no consciousness that is in a physical
form ;   this section a man must tread alone with his
Master ;   and beyond lies a section where a man is
alone with his God.

Not in one incarnation can this be achieved.
Three incarnations of absolute devotion without
error may serve ;   but who is without error, and how
far must we be upon the Path before absolute devotion is attained ?   We cannot step out of the march
of evolution with one foot and into the Cosmic
Light with the other ;   it takes many steps to tread
the Path, and some of them slip and have to be
retraced.   The difficulties are emphasised because
many embark lightheartedly upon this great and
terrible venture, but the fruits of it are not mini-
mised, for they transcend all that eye can see or
heart can dream.   Neither do we have to wait until
the end of the journey before we begin to reap.   Day
by day the manna fell during all the journey through
the wilderness, though Egypt had to be abandoned
and the Red Sea over-passed before it appeared.

So in the great journey of the soul to the Promised
Land, which is the Way of Initiation, the safety of
human habitations has to be left, and the soul
journeys houseless and alone into the wilderness
and comes to the Red Sea ; here it is that the weak
turn back and return into slavery to make bricks
without straw for which they receive no wages.
But if the supreme test of the Red Sea is faced,
the waves are parted by an unseen force and the
traveller passes through dry-shod, with a wall of
waters standing up on either hand ;   this is the test

of faith, for by mundane law those waters should fall; it is only a higher law that keeps them back.

Then, the test being safely passed, though still in the wilderness, waters flow from the rock and manna falls daily, for though still in the world of sense, the traveller has come under the operation of a higher law.

CHAPTER II

In order to understand the import of initiation it is necessary to glance at the history of the evolution of humanity. Occult science teaches that other species of human beings existed previously to humanity as we now know it; these distinct species it calls the Root Races, and believes that the Root Race at present in possession of the globe is the fifth in this evolutionary series. In the two previous races, known as the Polarian and Hyperborean, consciousness had not become individualised, but humanity was overshadowed by its group-soul in the same way that the lower types of animals are overshadowed to the present day. The esoteric psychology of the group-soul affords a vast field of study and is too involved to enter into in the present pages; it must suffice to say that the operations of such a group-soul may be recognised in the intelligence of the ant and bee and the migrations of the birds. Many puzzling phenomena of animal intelligence are accounted for by the hypothesis of a group-soul.

As human evolution proceeded, more and more of the mind-stuff common to the species became organised into distinct complexes and incarnated in the many separate vehicles which formed the composite body of the group; these organised complexes, developing about the original nuclei, or divine sparks, scattered through the amorphous mass of the group-soul, ultimately became individualised entities and developed into human form.   After evolution had proceeded a certain distance, these individualised entities attained a degree of independence which rendered them difficult of control by the over-shadowing group-soul ;   and the Logos summoned to His aid those of His children who had completed the cycle of their growth in a previous evolution and attained cosmic adulthood.   (For it must not be forgotten that an evolution is to the Solar Logos what an incarnation is to a human being ;   and that each evolution is but a day in the great cyclic life of Brahma.)

These Great Ones influenced the forerunners of humanity by presenting images to their minds by means of a process which we should call tele-pathic suggestion.   The images necessary to enable sensation to be translated into mentation were thus provided ready-made, as it were, and mankind was saved the lengthy and laborious necessity of build-ing these images out of accumulated experiences. In the first Cosmic Day, of course, the then human-ity had to go through this process ;   but subsequent evolutions were enabled rapidly to recapitulate stages previously gone through by the aid of their Elder Brethren ;   it is only after the high-water mark of the previous Cosmic Day has been reached that evolution has to take place out of the raw material of experience.

By means of the experiences to which conscious-ness had now rendered man susceptible, the con-crete or objective mind of humanity was gradually built up upon the basis of the inspirational content which had been injected into the subconscious human mind by the ministrations of the Elder Brethren and the influences of the group-soul. The point was finally reached when the concrete consciousness over-ruled the inspirational subconsciousness, just as the latter had over-ruled the influence of the group-mind ; the direct line of control from the Logos, through the Oversoul, to the individual, thus being lost. It therefore became necessary to link up the conscious mind with the subconscious mind so that the cosmic control might be re-established, and this was the function of the Cosmic Initiators, or Manus.

These Great Ones, who are the nearest kin to humanity of all the Lords of Evolution, having attained their development in the Cosmic Day immediately preceding our own, appeared upon the earth during the middle of the Atlantean Period. These are the " High Priests after the Order of Melchisedec," being without father or mother and building their physical vehicles without human assistance. It was their office to communicate with the concrete mind of humanity, and forge a connecting chain of associated ideas from consciousness to sub-consciousness, thereby enabling man to pick up the subtler vibrations which are the voice of the higher spheres.

In order to do this they had to appear to concrete consciousness in concrete form ; hence with infinite difficulty they had to build a vehicle that concrete consciousness could cognise. These anthropoid forms were so unsuited to the highly evolved forces they had to carry that they were only held together with the greatest difficulty and for short periods of time. Hence the accounts of the sudden appearances and disappearances of the gods which form

part of all primitive traditions. For these Great
Ones were the actual gods of myth and fable, the
Divine Founders of racial cultures to which all
primitive traditions look back. (They must not,
however, be confused with the personifications of the
nature forces of later periods ; these are the culture
gods or divine progenitors.)

These great entities gathered about themselves
bands of students selected from the most promising
of the race to which they came, and developed their
faculties until they were able to cognise consciously
those subtle types of vibration which hitherto they
had only been able to perceive intuitively, thus
recovering the primitive type of mentation upon a
higher arc. This having once been accomplished,
the Manus were able to withdraw to those planes
upon which they could function with greater ease and
freedom, summoning their pupils to " rise upon the
planes " and attend them there for instruction, and
leaving it to those same pupils to train others as
they themselves had been trained, thus recruiting
the occult school through succeeding generations.

Thus was the great Sun-worship of Atlantis
founded and its school of initiation equipped with
knowledge. The Manus were able to tell their pupils
of the formations of the spheres because they themselves had been present when the spheres were
being builded ; they could inform them of the
phases through which evolution had passed because
they were either eye-witnesses, having themselves
developed in certain of the phases, or were the
initiated pupils of those who had. Thus it is that
the occult schools hold the traditions of the history
of cosmic evolution.

CHAPTER III

READERS of esoteric literature will be aware that
there are many different schools of occultism, and
will find that the teachings and symbolism employed
in all are fundamentally the same; so much so that
by a mere translation of the terminology the initiate
of one is enabled to understand the scriptures of
another. Nevertheless, these schools are not identi-
cal, for although the form is the same owing to their
common origin, the force that animates them is
entirely different owing to the circumstances of
their foundation.

It will be remembered that, among the many
seismic disasters which shook ancient Atlantis, there
were three of greater magnitude than the others;
and these were distinguished as the Three Great
Cataclysms. Before each of these cataclysms an
emigration went forth of those who had sufficient
development to enable them to foresee the disaster.
These took with them copies of the Sacred Books,
and also had among them initiates of a grade to
found a lodge. These initiates drew their authority
for the foundation of the new centre from the then
Manu. Now the Manus, like all else, function
under the aspects of the cosmic phases, and as the
Logos of our system is a triune entity, whose three
phases are wisdom, power and love, the Logoidal

24

phases run through a cycle of three, so that although all three aspects are always there, yet at one time one, and at another time another, will predominate, just as a triangle, revolving upon its centre, would present first one angle, and then another, to the observer's gaze, while still remaining triangular. This sequence can be observed in history if a sufficiently lengthy period be studied ; there will be a phase in human culture during which power is being built up, succeeded by another in which wisdom is being accumulated, and culminating in the final phase of the period in which brotherly love brings in a Golden Age.

Thus it was that the force transmitted to their disciples by the Manus of Atlantis was coloured by the Logoidal aspect which prevailed at the time of their functioning. The force transmitted by a Manu is spoken of as his Ray. In addition to enabling man to raise his consciousness to awareness of the subtler planes, the Manus put their pupils in touch with a great cosmic force proceeding direct from the Logos, and it is with this force that candidates are put in touch by means of the ritual of their initiation. It will thus be seen that, although the theory taught to an initiate of the different occult schools is fundamentally the same, the *modus operandi* of its practice will differ greatly according to the special nature of the Ray which supplies what may metaphorically be called the motive power of the Order.

The great Sun Temple, in which all the Rays met, no longer exists, being sunk beneath the waters of the Atlantic, but its teaching is still preserved by the three great occult traditions which are the descendants of the three great emigrations.

The First Emigration, which came out under the direction of a Manu operating under the Power aspect of the Logoidal cycle, has power for its keynote. This emigration, moving eastward according to the then disposition of the land-masses of the globe, halting each year to sow and reap its wheat and building temporary altars where it did so, moved across the north of Europe and Asia, leaving a megalithic trail behind it, until its progress was blocked by what we now call the Yellow Sea ; it then spread southward along the coast-lands of Asia until it finally contacted the remains of the Lemurian culture in the Pacific, from which it derived some of those elements which render it to-day a dangerous and polluted current. Although it is not permissible in a paper of this nature to enter into questions which involve practical occultism, those who know the nature of the Sin of the Mindless may be able to deduce its results.

It is this First Emigration Tradition which is the basis of all the primitive cults of Ju-juism, Fantee-ism, and primitive magic ; its initiation is a Second Plane initiation, and gives its candidates access to the lower astral only. And although, because it is the plane of control for the physical plane, it is admittedly necessary to have the powers of this plane for any magical operations involving the manipulation of the etheric forces or dense matter, it is nevertheless essential that the occultist who essays the processes of this plane should hold the initiations of the plane above, from which it in its turn is controlled ; otherwise he will tend to become absorbed into its conditions, and as the initiation of the second plane employs a very primitive type of force which can only have an uplifting influence upon a type of intelligence so lowly that it is, at the present stage of evolution, sub-human, to place oneself under the control of these forces is a regression for a civilised man. Upon this plane the white man must function as a master; he cannot, with justice to himself, meet its entities upon equal terms. The phenomena which characterise the magic of this plane are those with which the experiments of the séance room have made us familiar, and in view of the foregoing words, the reader can readily see wherein lies the danger of these researches in the hands of the ignorant and inexperienced.

The Second Great Emigration moved in a more southerly latitude, owing to the advance of the Polar ice, and, crossing Central Europe, continued its easterly movement till its course was barred by the uplands of Asia with their eternal snows. Here the temples were established, forming the Himalayan Centre; and from here the culture spread down the river valleys, following the waterways, as primitive travel must; so that all those parts of the world whose rivers have their rise in the ranges of Central Asia likewise look to the Himalayan centre for the inspiration of their religion. From this emigration it is that the Wisdom Religions of the East are derived, and although some of the sects are tainted by the influences of the First Emigration culture, over which in parts the second outpouring flowed (just as the first was tainted by the lingering Lemurian tradition), yet for the most part a remarkable degree of purity has been maintained in the inner Orders, and some of the profoundest knowledge in the world is guarded in its mountain strongholds.

The Third Great Emigration came out from the doomed continent immediately before the final cataclysm sank it for ever below the waves; and, travelling eastward in a yet more southerly direction than its two predecessors, crossed northern Africa and continued its journey till " the Red Sea and the Wilderness" barred its way, and it settled down upon the only fertile lands of that barren region, the valley and delta of the Nile, founding the culture which is known to us as Egyptian. Anyone who compares the Egyptian civilisation with that of Central America, which tradition states to have been an outlying portion of Atlantis, cannot fail to be struck by the similarity of the two, whether shown in the concepts of their religion or their architecture.

Navigation developed early in the inland sea, and wherever the galleys went in trade the Egyptian philosophy penetrated, so that the Third Emigration Tradition spread all over the Mediterranean Basin and the Near East. The Tyrrian and Grecian Mysteries admit that their adepts were trained in the Egyptian temples; from the Tyrrian we know that the Hebrew tradition derived its renaissance, and from the Grecian Mysteries grew that Gnosis which translated the spiritual concepts of Christianity into the language of the intellect; and from the Gnosis, crushed as it was by the Christian Church after the power had passed into the hands of those who knew nothing but the outer form of the truth they held, arose that long line of intellectual mystics who kept the fire alight in Europe and whom later generations have called the Alchemists.

As the development of communications caused cultures to spread and overflow each other, it was natural that the lines of demarcation between one tradition and another should not be as rigid in later days as they were in the earlier; and the disciples of the second and third Traditions met and influenced each other along the trade routes of the Near East; but though the teachings may have undergone modifications under the influence of characteristic racial cultures, the forces employed in initiations are distinct. The disciplines, or methods of training, are also radically different. Those of the Power Ray work from below upwards, and by operating upon objects of the plane of manifestation, seek to influence their subtle aspects.

It is characteristic of the methods of this Ray that they are obliged to have a material starting-point, a magical substance, which is their *point d'appui*; and much of their wisdom consists in a knowledge of those natural objects which are in close association with the unseen world and thereby give ready ingress to it; and we see the witch-doctors of these cults with collections of curious trophies, each of which is credited with supernatural values.

Whether their values depend upon their actual properties or upon the faith of their owner is a point which has to be tested in each individual case, for there is too much evidence of the existence of such properties for all claims to be dismissed as delusion, and it is a rash man who will undertake to give an opinion upon a matter which he has not investigated.

In this tradition, then, we find much knowledge of physical magic, and of those drugs which affect states of consciousness by acting on the nervous system and endocrines, and at the same time a complete dearth of any rational understanding of the methods used. First Tradition knowledge, when uninfluenced by the more evolved traditions, is a rule-of-thumb affair, and much adulterated by pure superstition, which is as alien to true occult science as it is to natural science.

The Second Tradition methods are characterised by the stress laid upon the acquisition of knowledge, and the very remarkable systems of mind culture whereby the consciousness of the initiate is expanded; at the same time, however, the teachers of this school are not ignorant of the First Tradition methods, by reason of the fact that, arising from the same Atlantean school of occultism, though at a later period of its history, they were in possession of the lower as well as the higher degrees that evolution had added; they had all which the initiates of the First Emigration had possessed as well as the acquirements of later generations, and the original methods, being fundamentally sound, have never been superseded upon the planes to which they belong. Each tradition, in fact, possesses all that its predecessor possessed, in addition to that which is characteristically its own.

The Western Esoteric Tradition had its origin in the third and last Emigration from Atlantis, which took place immediately before the final catastrophe which sank the Lost Continent beneath the sea, together with its wisdom and civilisation. The priests who accompanied the emigration bore with them the Sacred Books and Symbols so that they might found a Temple of the Sun in the Land of Darkness towards which they made their way. For the founding of this temple they received a mandate from the then Manu, and the contact, being when the Love Aspect of the Logos prevailed, was consequently upon the Ray of love and devotion; and just as the First Emigration, coming out under the Power Aspect of the Logos, had for its ideal the wielding of power, perfect and supreme beneath the cosmic laws; and the Second Emigration, coming out under the Wisdom Aspect of the Logos, had perfected wisdom for its ideal; so the Third and last Emigration, coming out under the Love Aspect of the Logos, had brotherhood and compassion for its ideals and socialisation for its task.

The priests of the Third Emigration, being trained in the same tradition that had sent forth the priests of the First and Second, possessed the secret wisdom of both these traditions in addition to that which later ages had evolved; and through these phases the new Mystery School had to pass in building up its system, as can be clearly distinguished in the history of the Mysteries; but having recapitulated these, and reached a level of culture equivalent to that of the parent civilisation, the last and characteristic phase was brought in by the work of the Master Jesus. The Western Tradition therefore has three aspects: the Nature aspect, corresponding to the Astral initiations, whose master on the Lower Astral is represented by the Left-hand pillar of the Temple, and on the Upper Astral by Orpheus, the sweet singer; the Wisdom aspect, corresponding to the initiations of the mind, whose Master on the Lower Mental Plane is Hermes, and on the Upper Mental is Euclid; and the Devotional and Spiritual Aspect, whose Master of Masters is Jesus of Nazareth. These three great aspects form the full Western Tradition, and each without the other two is but partial.

Unless the Ray of Nature Worship is complemented by the Ray of Intellectual Development and Hermetic Training, sub-human aspects will become

dominant in the sub-consciousness of the aspirant ;
and unless the Intellectual Ray be illuminated by
the spirituality of the Devotional Ray, it will tend
to hardness of heart and narrowness of outlook ;
while the Nature Ray itself sweetens and vivifies
the Mysteries with the joy and beauty of its primitive nature-contacts.

All Rays unite in the sun; and therefore their
paths converge, and after a certain stage is reached
they coalesce, so that an initiate of the higher degrees
of any mystery school will stand upon common
ground with the initiates of any other school ; but
in the lower degrees, and especially in their methods
of work on the astral and physical planes, the
schools are widely divergent, as the differences in
their invocations testify.   That which summons the
devas of the East will not invoke the angelic hosts
of the West, nor will the banishing formula which
sends Hindu devils about their business give protection in a European country, as many an English
chela has found to his cost.   The very mantrams,
spells and Words of Power are put together upon
different principles.   To borrow a metaphor from
music, the Rays are played in different keys, and if
transposition is to be effected, it must be done by a
skilled master who understands the correspondences ;
horrible effects are produced by merely playing
sharps as flats.

Any student of comparative religion knows that
although the great deities can be identified throughout the different mythologies, and analogous symbols
appear in all religious systems, modification in
both names and signs takes place when they are
translated from one country to another.   Many
students ignore the differences and concentrate

upon the similarity, believing the alterations to be due to local peculiarities of pronunciation, and therefore superficial, and that having identified the different sun-gods throughout the world, they are dealing with one and the same potency. It is, of course, quite true that the same force is behind all of them, but one might just as well attempt to use indiscriminately a telephone, a dynamo, and an electric cautery because the same force is behind them all.

The correct pronunciation and orthography of Words of Power is extremely important in all occult operations, and they do not undergo permutation without reason, but according to definite laws. The change in the Sacred Names from country to country is to make the forces fit the conditions, and is not lightly to be tampered with.

Occultism upon the planes of form is always racial and local because it must be adapted to its environment; and although upon the higher planes one formula is valid for all, and mystic experiences of the same type characterise all the higher degrees so that adepts can meet upon an equal footing, the systems employed in training aspirants are totally different and should never be confounded. Meditation and asceticism will bring the Eastern chela to the feet of his Master, but the Western initiator, working in the much denser material conditions of that civilisation, has to employ ritual to get his results—rituals that very few Eastern bodies could stand. The meditative methods of the East will not get results in the West unless the vitality is lowered, and it is a very risky thing to attempt to handle high potencies on a lowered vitality; nor will the aspirant fare well in the rush and drive of our civilisation.

Methods worked out to fit one type of life, régime and etheric conditions, are not suitable for another and totally different type, and the unsuitability shows itself in the nervous strain of the pupil. If you wish to follow the yogi methods you must lead the yogi life ; if you do not, you will break down.

The Eastern forces require very purified and rarefied vehicles for their operation, and therefore the primitive aspects of the nature have to be pruned away. The Western forces are much stronger and more drastic in their action, because they take hold of the primitive aspects and use them for their own ends, sublimating the base metal into gold, not precipitating the gold from the ether. You may enable yourself to receive wireless signals beyond normal range either by increasing the power of the transmitting apparatus or the sensitivity of the receiving apparatus. The Western method employs the former, the Eastern the latter. If the teacher desires to use the methods of the East, he must make his pupils fulfil the conditions of the East, and for the higher degrees he must go to the East.

The Western methods are based upon the Western symbolism and potencies ; they have their roots deep in the spiritual life of the race. Their influences have moulded its civilisation, and therefore they do not tend to make their initiates aliens in their own land and unfit them for the conditions of European life ; but rather they train their aspirants to co-operate with racial forces, to use, and to be used by them.

The knowledge of the Ancient Wisdom of the East has been popularised by the Theosophical Society, but do not let us forget that there is our own native esotericism hidden in the superconscious mind of the race, and that we have our holy places at our very doors which have been used for initiations from time immemorial, potent alike for the nature contacts of the Celt, the work of the Hermetist, and the mystical experiences of the Church of the Holy Grail.

CHAPTER IV

THE Western Tradition has several different aspects which really constitute schools within the Tradition, and these are generally spoken of as the Rays. These Rays are generally named after the colours of the spectrum with which they are held to equate. There is some difference of opinion concerning the colour-notation to be assigned to the Rays; the popular system of assigning the first Ray to the first Plane, and so on, is purely arbitrary and exoteric, for the Planes did not develop in a single Ray-cycle, periods of Pralaya intervening at different points. The true esoteric colour-notation differs from this in several respects. A terminology has therefore been employed which names the Rays according to the school which saw their highest development, and correlates them with the planes and the states of consciousness. This is a system which will be readily understood by readers whatever may be the terminology they are accustomed to, and prevents the confusion of mind which arises when the terms to which one is habituated are given an unfamiliar implication.

The subject of the Rays is highly technical and intricate, and although it is of great importance in practical occultism, it is not possible to enter upon it in detail in these pages, for it demands a book to itself. It must suffice to say that the Rays originate in the periodic outpourings of the Logoidal life-impulse. These outpourings may be conceived of as cutting channels on the inner planes, and the Logoidal force continues to flow in these channels after the original spate has spent itself. These outpourings build up the successive planes of manifestation, depositing them, one might say, as the river-flood deposits silt. Each of these outpourings has to find its ingress into the plane of matter through the consciousness of an incarnated being, and the Great Ones, perfected in previous evolutions, come forward in turn to undertake this task. After they have completed it, and the spate, having deposited its silt, is subsiding, they withdraw to the Inner Planes, and there continue their work of focussing that particular manifestation of the Logoidal Life and giving it form and expression. They are then known as the Lords of the Rays or Star Logoi.

The planes of human consciousness correspond with the planes laid down by the Rays, and it is the forces of a Ray, re-concentrated to a miniature spate by means of a ritual, which are used to stimulate the corresponding plane of consciousness into active functioning.

Each soul possesses all seven aspects, but in a given incarnation some of these may be latent. There is very seldom an even, all-round development. One of these planes will be the focus of consciousness and the other aspects will be subordinate and contributory thereto. For instance, one person may function in his emotions and his judgment will be swayed by his feelings. Another may concentrate on his mind, and, in the old phrase, his head will rule his heart. When these folk come to initiation it is the difficult task of the initiator to try and persuade them to develop the complement- tary aspects and so effect a balance.

It is a comparatively easy matter to induce a stimulation of the natural bent of a person. The difficulty is to induce a corresponding strengthening of his weak points, which alone will produce balance. The man who focusses in his mind has to learn to use his heart, and the man who focusses in his heart has to learn to use his head. Neither alone is sufficient.

Students, therefore, tend to separate themselves into groups according to type, and the different types have to be dealt with differently in the initiation school. The Lesser Mysteries aim at giving an all-round preliminary training, first in the purification and discipline of character, and then in the development of the intellectual powers, especially that of concentration. All candidates need to pass through this course, and many failures come from too early specialisation. It is only after they have passed through the three grades in which consciousness is trained that the dedication is offered and accepted and they pass on to the Greater Mysteries.

Here it is that they are separated out on to the Rays, working upon first one and then another till they have acquired the Powers of the Planes to which the Rays correspond. Each Ray influences a different aspect of consciousness, and by the time the student has passed through them all, his nature will be developed, purified and harmonised in all its aspects; then according to his temperament he chooses the Ray in which he will specialise, and thereafter settles down to his work upon that Ray;

but it is essential that he shall have had experience of all the Rays before he does this, otherwise he will be like a composer who is trying to score a band-piece and does not understand the technique of the wood-wind; he cannot score for an instrument unless he understands its technique. So with the initiate: even if his chosen plane be the Upper Spiritual, he will need to have knowledge of the Lower Astral; and if his chosen plane be the powerful elemental forces of the Lower Astral, he will need none the less the contacts of the Upper Spiritual lest he be drawn under and submerged in the non-human aspects of nature.

Each plane and its corresponding aspect of consciousness is opened up under the ægis of the Lord of the Ray, whose name is the supreme Word of Power of that Plane.

Each occult school, unfortunately, tends to specialise, because racial temperaments have their natural bent. The Rays most worked at present in the Western Tradition are the Rays of the Concrete Mind, and of the Concrete Spirit. The Eastern Tradition, on the other hand, has brought to a high degree of development the Ray of the Etheric aspect of matter in the Hatha Yoga, and the Ray of the Abstract Spirit in the Raja Yoga. Other Rays have had their development in different phases of the world's history. The Greeks, for instance, worked their initiations on the Rays of the Upper Astral and the Abstract Mind. When we come to study a Ray, therefore, we turn to the esoteric school which specialised in that aspect.

The seventh plane, the Plane of Abstract Spirit, is never contacted at the present stage of evolution while in the body; the ego must withdraw from the body for that contact, and the body then goes into deep trance. This aspect has been most highly developed in the East, and therefore this Ray is generally known as the Buddhic Ray ; but we have examples of it in the West in our ecstatics; St. Theresa is our principal authority upon it. It is exceedingly rare at the present day, and can only be developed in retreat under ascetic conditions. It has no Ray Logos in the sense in which the other Rays have, for it has not yet been brought through into manifestation in matter, and therefore has never focussed through the consciousness of an incarnated being. Its invocation and contacts are those of the Holy Ghost, and it is never operated in waking consciousness, but only, as has already been said, in full trance.

The operations of these contacts involve the withdrawal of the soul from the world, and are never undertaken until the time is approaching when freedom from the Wheel of Birth and Death may be claimed. Concentration on this contact before the time is ripe causes an arrestation of spiritual growth. We have an example of this in Europe in the Quietists : Mme. Guyon, to use an expressive metaphor from Evelyn Underhill's great work on Mysticism, " basked like a cat in the rays of the Sun of Life." It is the extensive development of this aspect that has paralysed the progress of the East.

The sixth plane, or Plane of Concrete Spirit, is the focussing point of civilisation at present. Hereon are developed the spiritual qualities of Love, Truth, Goodness, Purity, and many others. This Ray was made manifest to man by the Master Jesus, who is its Master of Masters, its Ray Logos ; it is therefore known as the Christian Ray. The initiation of this Ray is the highest ideal which a man can achieve while still remaining on the human path of evolution.

It is the contacts of this Ray which give the saint his Vision Beautiful and which make the chalice into the Graal. It is the hidden power of Christianity which was taught to the disciples in the Upper Room whilst the multitude received but a rule of life—a rule, however, which, if faithfully followed, would bring them to that Upper Room where they could receive the inner teaching which is not withheld, but merely kept separate. It is the power of the Christian Ray that shines through the Graal; and it is to the Church of the Graal that the aspirant comes who elects to follow the Way of the Cross. This is the Church behind the church which is not seen, but realised; it is to this that devotion to the Sacraments brings a man. The church which is of stone fades away for him, and he finds himself in the Church not built with hands, eternal in the heavens. It is here that the Christian mystic worships; here that he meets his Master face to face in the wine and bread that are not bread and wine, but the substances of a magical operation sublimated to spiritual gold.

The initiations of the Plane of Abstract Mind are concerned with the development of intuitive thinking and of the power of deductive reasoning to extend from the known into the Unknown and translate it into cognisable terms. It is often called the Pythagorean Ray, because it had its heyday in the Mystery Schools of Greece. This is the true Wisdom Ray, for its contacts represent the first of the objective initiations, wherein the doors of self are opened and it enters into immediate relations with the Not-self. All initiations prior to this do but open up the hidden heights and depths of the self.

The Ray of the Concrete Mind is the highest aspect of the incarnate personality. Thrice-greatest Hermes is its Ray Logos. Its highest development was in the Egyptian and Cabalistic systems, and it was blended with Christian thought in the schools of the Neo-platonists and the Gnostics; but the persecuting energy of the Church, long since exotericised, stamped it out as an organised system. Its studies were only kept alive during the Dark Ages among the Jews, who were the chief exponents of its Cabalistic aspect. Its Egyptian aspect was reintroduced into Europe by the Templars after the Crusades had put them in touch with the Holy Centres in the Near East. Stamped out again by the fear and jealousy of the Church, it reappeared once more in the long line of Alchemists who flourished after the power of Rome was broken by the Reformation; and it is still alive to-day.

The Ray which correlates with the Upper Astral Plane is known as the Celtic Ray, for its initiation of the higher emotional self gave the Celtic racial culture its impetus. It is seen in its highest mani-festation in the earlier Greek tradition, especially in the Dionysian cults before the influence of Eastern and Egyptian thought had produced developments which were not typical of the Hellenic racial genius.

The Celtic Ray is essentially elemental and deals with the nature aspect of things; being an initia-tion of the emotions, its standards of value are æsthetic, not ethical; its ideals are beauty and joy, not truth and goodness, and we must bear this in mind when judging its votaries. It is far removed from the world of men and mundane values; but without its leaven, utilitarianism would crush out the wider vision.

It is from this Ray that all imaginative work derives its inspiration and creative artists draw their power. It is essentially the Artist's Ray, whatever be the medium in which his craftsmanship finds expression ; and it is the force of this Ray which makes the subtle difference between the products of the handcraft worker and the products of the machine, and gives handmade things the subtle fascination they have for the sensitive soul. Even though their technique be not so perfect as that of the factory, they are alive with the wonderful elemental life of the Celtic Ray which their maker, working with creative inspiration drawn from that Ray, builds into them. Yes, they are literally alive, being ensouled with elemental essence, and hence they are " companionable " in a way that a machine-made object is not.

But although the Greek expression of the Ancient Wisdom affords excellent material for study, it is by means of the form it has built itself in the group-spirit of our race that we must seek to approach the actual contacts of its power, and the true expression of the Celtic Ray for the inhabitant of the British Isles is in the Gaelic fairy lore.

Many generations of British intellect have been nourished upon the classical tradition, and consequently have produced that remote, antique and alien type of artistic or literary beauty which is called classical. This is a type of beauty for whose appreciation a special culture is required, a classical culture similar to that which inspired the creator of the beautiful thing, because the elemental life which ensouls his creations is derived from the Hellenic aspect of the Celtic Ray (for the Roman tradition also derives from that source), and therefore it does not appeal to the common man who has not built up these contacts within his soul. Contacts with an alien force have to be slowly and elaborately built, they do not arise spontaneously, nor are they innate ; and not only must they be built, but they must be tenderly cherished, for they are tropical plants of the soul.

But that which derives from our native folk tradition springs up like water from the soil, made alive by the good brown earth and fresh with the breath of herb and tree ; it springs, it sparkles, and the wayfaring man, though dull, cannot but rejoice therein, for it is native to him ; he needs no commentary to tell him its beauties ; he loves it because he enjoys it ; and he enjoys it because it vitalises his nature. It vitalises his nature because it puts him in touch with the sun-warmed, rain-wet earth, his native earth, that his bare feet trod as a child when his soul was open and he still could feel the Unseen. It blows through his soul like the wind on high places ; it drives over him like the waves of the open sea ; and his heart leaps to it like the springing, leaping flames of the living fire ; for by the dust of his fathers he is kin to the elements in his native land, and by the road of his childhood dreams he approaches the Celtic contact. For the initiate of the Celtic Ray is the Immortal Child, the Fool of Heaven, ever young but never wise, for Wisdom is not upon the Celtic Ray.

The Ray which corresponds to the Lower Astral Plane is known as the Norse Ray, because the purest contacts of this much-corrupted tradition which are available to us in the West are those of the Nordic mythology. The Lower Astral Plane is the plane of the primitive instincts and the crude passions associated with them, and it is the sublimation of these passions which gives the ecstasy of the initiation of this contact. In the Nordic tradition, the ecstasy is derived from a sublimation of the quality of courage in its apotheosis as the baresark lust of battle.

In other traditions this Ray takes different forms. In the Hindu system it is the terrible Kali-worship, with its thugs and self-mutilations; the apotheosis of cruelty, not of courage. The Priapic, as distinguished from the Dionysian aspect of phallic worship, is also contacted on this Ray.

It must not be thought that this Ray is evil in itself, however. Nothing that God has created is evil in itself; it is only in its perversion and distortion that it becomes evil. The Norse Ray is the Ray of the heroic virtues of courage, endurance and stability. When this potent primitive element is lacking, people become decadent and neurotic, cranks and faddists, artificiality taking the place of the natural instincts.

The time when this Ray manifested upon earth is so remote that its functions correlate with the cerebellum, for it was in function before the cerebrum, the part of the brain which gives the characteristic human forehead, was developed. Normally, the mentation corresponding to this part of the brain does not come within the focus of the waking personality, but is sub-conscious, only rising to the surface during periods of intense emotion, or when the more recently developed parts of the brain have been put out of action by the influence of drugs or disease.

It is, of course, the Ray *par excellence* of Black Magic, and has become much contaminated in consequence. Its contacts are only used in primitive witch-cults and, contradictory as it may appear, by very highly-trained occultists ; for upon the ability to contact and control the forces of this plane depends the power to produce tangible effects in dense matter. The Name of the Master of Masters of this plane cannot be given, because it is a Word of Power, but it may be said that it is the special function of the Archangel Michael to guard the gates of the Underworld, so that no uprush of " chaos and old night " may break through on to the earth-plane.

The Ray which was concerned with the laying down of the Plane of Earth is of even greater antiquity than the Nordic Ray. It manifested before matter as known to us in its dense aspect had been evolved. As an initiatory force it develops the powers of the etheric double. Its contacts are worked in the East in the Hatha Yoga discipline, and as we have no corresponding school in the West, we will call it the Etheric Ray.

In its original aspect it has long since passed out of manifestation, but the cycle of evolution is beginning to bring it in again on a higher arc, and we are seeing a great development of the power of mind over body in such cults as Christian Science and the New Thought movement. It is, of course, by operating upon the etheric double that the mind-healer obtains his results, just as the fakir obtains his phenomena.

These seven Rays constitute the gamut of initiation, and no one can be justly called an adept who does not possess the degrees corresponding to them. The Buddhic Ray lies ahead of evolution ; the Etheric Ray in its original aspect lies behind it. The Christian Ray is the focussing point in the present age. It is along the lines laid down by the Master Jesus that development is taking place. The powers of other Rays, with the exception of the Buddhic Ray, which does not belong to the Earth-plane at present, are recapitulations whereby a man takes possession for himself of that which humanity has achieved in the past and which is part of the heritage of humanity.

The Master Jesus, Star Logos of the Ray under which modern civilisation is developing, is the Lord of this epoch, and His Name is the Supreme Word of Power, for to each manifestation·of the Christ are committed all things in heaven and earth, including those of His Brethren who have preceded Him in office. Another incarnation of the Christ-force will come in due evolutionary season, as all religions teach, but it has not come yet, and until it does the Master Jesus is the Master of Masters for the West and the Great Initiator of the white peoples.

CHAPTER V

MUCH has been written of recent years concerning Those who are called the Masters, and many different opinions have been expressed. Some writers rank Them as but little inferior to the Deity, and others seem to use the word as being equivalent to the "control" of the spiritualist, or even refer to Them as in human form and having places of residence on the physical plane. This has led to much misunderstanding and to a cheapening of the concept of these Divine Beings and supermen with whom it is possible for humanity to come into touch. The misunderstanding is largely due to the fact that all superhumanity has frequently been classed together by thoughtless students, and the functions of the Adept, the Master, and the Master of Masters, Star Logos, or Ray Chohan (according to the terminology employed) have been confused and their gradations confounded. In the terminology employed in these pages the word Master is never applied to a being incarnated on the physical plane, but is reserved for Those who no longer need to incarnate for the performance of Their work. The term Adept is used for those beings who have passed beyond the stage which evolution has as yet reached on our planet, and have therefore nothing to learn from its conditions, but elect to incarnate for the purpose of performing certain work; and they are not regarded as Divine Beings, but as elder brethren. The man or woman who has advanced beyond a certain grade in the Greater Mysteries is referred to as an initiate, and below these come the grades of brother, neophyte, dedicand, server, and seeker.

As the degrees of the hierarchy have reference to evolutionary stages, their significance can be best understood by studying them in their sequence, beginning at the first manifestation, which is now the highest, each subsequent advent bringing initiation a stage further down the planes ; and as humanity is meanwhile steadily evolving up the planes, there comes a time when cosmic consciousness can be attained and maintained in the normal waking state. " In my flesh shall I see God." The work of the Manus, the evolved of previous evolutions, has been explained in another chapter, and we will take up the story at the point where the Greater Masters, who were the pupils of the Manus, come into function.

Let us consider first the condition of humanity at the time the Manus began to appear upon the physical plane. It was far lower than that of the most primitive savage, intelligence being essentially animal in type, for it was the function of the Manus to assist in the development of those faculties which are characteristically human and distinguish us from our younger brethren, the animals. The Manus Themselves had evolved in previous evolutions ; and it was Their function to assist humanity rapidly to recapitulate the evolutionary experiences which should bring them abreast of the level at which their predecessors withdrew from the physical plane, so that humanity should take up the work of the planet where the Lords of Mind laid it down. In order to save the time occupied by a laborious rebuilding, certain of the perfected entities of the previous life-wave undertook the task of handing over to humanity the fruits of their evolution.

Humanity had only reached the stage of perceptive consciousness; that is to say, it could form mental images which were linked in memory-sequences; it had now become necessary that conceptive consciousness should be developed, so that memory-images could be synthesised into generalisations. The Manus, by means of suggestion or thought-transference, planted IDEAS in human consciousness, and the men chosen for this operation, once having experienced the apprehension of a concept and realised the possibility of this form of thought, were soon able to construct other syntheses of images for themselves, and they were made assiduously to practise this process under their instructors, just as aspirants at the present time are made to practise the intuitional thought of the abstract planes.

Once this process was well under way, the Manus were able to withdraw to a higher plane, and the pupils They had initiated into Their methods of thought were left to train their fellows under the instructions of the Manus. In due course of evolution some of these pupils had made so much progress that they had evolved beyond the need of incarnation, and themselves withdrew from the physical plane. The Lords of Mind who had been their initiators were then able to withdraw to Their own place, which is not on our planet, though within the limits of our solar system, and the Lords of Humanity became the initiators of Their own people.

The perfected entities evolved by previous evolutions have their own functions within the universe as laws, forces and principles, the Lords of Mind alone approximating in the least degree to our concept of conscious beings. Though perfect and complete according to their own type, they are of a much lower grade of evolution than humanity will be when it has in its turn completed its course. But just as a dog of two years old is in a much higher state of development than a child of two years old, and might be put to guard the latter, so the Lords of Mind are infinitely higher than the infant humanity, though humanity will be higher than the Lords of Mind when fully evolved.

As each fresh phase of human evolution was entered upon, one of the Lords of Humanity undertook to incarnate upon the physical plane in order to introduce into human consciousness the archetypal ideas which it was intended to work out during that phase, and these He taught to a chosen band of disciples by precept, but to the multitude by example ; that is to say, He lived the ideal life, He manifested the ideal character, thus presenting a new concept of human perfection to men's consciousness, and forming a standard against which they could measure their lives and actions. They are thus the Great Exemplars, and represent the Archetypal Man to which humanity attains when it has completed the phase of evolution thus ushered in.

But They are more than Exemplars, They are also Saviours, for before the work of a new phase can be undertaken they have to clear up and adjust any residuum of error in the last phase of evolution, and this They do by taking upon Themselves the sin of the world, to use theological terminology.

There is known to occultists a method of healing by substitution, in which, by extreme compassion with the suffering of a beloved one, the suffering is experienced in the very self, and then, by the appropriate reaction and realisation, is expiated upon a higher plane. Such a process is extremely dangerous, for, if the expiation is not successfully accomplished, the would-be healer is left with the disease; it is also an extremely painful process, for what would have been the long-drawn-out physical suffering of the patient is transmuted into its equivalent of mental suffering in the healer for a short period, and therefore concentrated. Moreover, the whole process has to be accomplished according to the laws of karma, or more harm than good is done.

Now that which is sometimes done between two individuals is performed between the Saviour and the group-soul of the world when an Atonement is made at the end of a phase of evolution. In the few short hours of the Crucifixion the sin and suffering left over from a phase of evolution were realised and abreacted. Little wonder that, in anticipation of this ordeal, the Lord of the Purple Ray prayed, " Let this cup pass from me."

The initiate of the Western tradition gives to the Passion and its ritual presentation in the Mass the same place that the theologian does; to him the Eucharist represents the supreme contact of his Ray and race. But he also recognises the other great Redeemers, and knows that the legend of the sacrificial death is true of all of Them.

When a Master has incarnated as Redeemer and passed through the sacrificial death, *He does not reincarnate*, but becomes the Star Logos of His Ray, one of the Seven Spirits before the throne, and he brings that aspect of Logoidal force to a focus through the lens of His personification. Now a personification is not the same as a personality, but is the image which the individuality builds of a particular incarnation in order to manifest upon the plane of matter. This is a significant point in practical occultism, and is what Madame Blavatsky refers to when she says in "The Secret Doctrine" that a Master's body is illusory. When psychics report that the Master Jesus is incarnated at the present time at such-and-such a place, it is not an incarnation they have perceived, but a personification, a thought-form in the consciousness of the Star Logos which is being used to focus His Ray; and when this incarnation is reported at a Sacred Centre in the Himalayas or the Caucasus, it means that the astral body of the seer is working at one of those astral centres. It is not that the Master Jesus is living there, but that the psychic is functioning there! A very different matter. It is an extremely easy thing to get the astral consciousness reopening when the seer is supposed to be functioning in his causal, or abstract, mental body, and then both types of consciousness are presented simultaneously to the ego, like two exposures of one photographic plate.

Again, psychics who have not got the proper testing-formulæ for " trying the spirits " on the plane and Ray on which they are working, may easily find the subconscious content externalised as thought-forms, and so merely be reading their own sub-conscious minds when they believe themselves to be reading the Records, thereby bringing through pre-conceived notions as vision.

Finally, a psychic who can work no higher than the astral plane will describe everything in terms of anthropomorphic picture-consciousness ; when therefore he or she elects to investigate things which are not of that plane, they cannot rise consciously to a realisation of the abstract, but will only be able to see the reflections in the astral light, using astral consciousness as a mirror ; and things which are of pure spirit, and therefore formless, will be reported as having form and their appearance described. The appearances seen are simply symbolic representations of the abstract as apprehended by concrete consciousness, which the seer should be able to interpret in abstract terms, as did Anna Kingsford in regard to her illuminations ; but when we get a seer who does not understand the method of the transmutation of symbolism between the planes, we get an account of the Christ standing under a tree in His garden and blessing the world with outstretched hands every evening.

Now the Christ is not, and never has been, a personality ; it is not even individualised, but is simply the regenerative and reconciling aspect of the Logoidal force, and as such is spoken of as the Cosmic Christ in order to distinguish it from the manifestation of that force coming through the channel of a Redeemer's consciousness. It is this force that has functioned through all the World Saviours, Eastern, or Western, but Jesus the Christ, being the Saviour of the Western civilisation phase of evolution, is for us " the only Name under heaven whereby we shall be saved," that is to say, whereby we shall obtain the supreme initiation available at present to us in this sphere. "To each man his own Master," nor may we "judge another man's servant," but to the Western races Jesus of Nazareth is The Christ, for it is His ideal that our civilisation is so slowly and laboriously working out. The Coming World Teacher concerns the next root race, and has nothing to do with Western civilisation, which must work out the Law of Love according to the dispensation of the Master Jesus. It is only the seed-people of the new race who will follow the new Teacher when He summons them, and they will not find it possible to regenerate European civilisation by the methods they wish to inaugurate, but will have to segregate themselves into colonies or communities and live their own life apart, while Western civilisation works out its own destiny and achieves its zenith; then, with the decay of that civilisation, the souls which it has perfected will withdraw, later to reincarnate in the new root race; but they will come as individuals, for it is not possible to transfer the group-soul of a civilisation from one Manu to another; for the group-soul, like the group-body, or social organisation, is finite and mortal, and must die before it can be reincarnated; it is the spirit of humanity alone which is immortal and endures through an evolution; the spirit alone which is universal and one throughout the planet. Social organisations are as separate as individuals, and their group-souls, or devas, will not let them coalesce, though they may form brotherhoods upon the plane of group consciousness.

The Master Jesus is "an High Priest after the Order of Melchisedec," and had, according to the Western Esoteric Tradition, but two manifestations on this plane before He passed beyond the planes of form after the third, last and highest manifestation which was the completion of His work. He was never of our humanity, and is now of the grade of Cosmic Fire in the hierarchy, and therefore the sun is His appropriate symbol and His Church keeps the seasons of the solar year and identifies them with the incidents of His career, thus giving rise to the hypothesis of the Solar Myth.

The Gospel stories deal with two sets of facts, the historical narrative of the Incarnation, and the attributes of the office of Redeemer, which our Lord held; the exposition of this dual significance would be too long for the present pages, but the enlightened will readily be able to distinguish the two, and allocate each incident in the divine Life to its proper category.

The Master Jesus is not of the same hierarchical grade with other of the Masters with whom He has sometimes been associated or confused. He stands upon the same degree as the Manus Krishna and Osiris, as a Master of Masters upon His Ray, below Whom are the Greater Masters, Who are Regenerators, but not Redeemers, for they did not die the Sacrificial Death. Of these are Moses, who gave the Law to Israel, Gautama, who gave the Law to Asia, Mohammed, who gave the Law to Africa, and Paul, who gave the Law to Europe. The work of these is done with the conscious minds of men, but the work of the Christs is done with the consciousness of the race.

Below these again are the Lesser Masters, who in Christian terminology would be called the saints, and it is these who have to do with the teaching and training of humanity at the present time.

The mystic talks of the Communion of Saints, and the occultist talks of the Lodge of the Masters, and both refer to different types of the same thing. The Communion of Saints is that body of " just men made perfect " who, by the Way of the Cross, have passed beyond incarnation. And as they loved the Church during their sojourn in the tabernacle of flesh, so they still love her in the life of the spirit. And so, "with angels, archangels, and all the company of heaven " they answer the summons of the sanctus bell, and in that Mass of the Grail of which the mystical soul partakes, the Church of Heaven and Earth meet together. It is they who constitute the Church behind the church, or, in the language of the Western Tradition, the Church of the Grail, and it is in this " body of just men made perfect " that the strength of the Church lies.

It is for this reason that prayer to the saints and the adoption of a patron saint has great value upon the Mystic Way, for his Patron Saint is to the mystic what his Master is to the occultist—a lens through which the Cosmic Power is concentrated, a symbol by which consciousness is lifted to transcendent concepts, an Elder Brother who, having come by the same path, understands the human needs of the seeker committed to his care, and out of a deeper wisdom and greater power can give counsel and help in those small things which seem so big to the struggling soul.

Great cosmic forces are only used for great cosmic purposes, but those cosmic souls whom we call Saint and Master can transmute and apply these forces for the relief of the little human needs of those in Their care in a way which those souls themselves, owing to the smallness of their grasp and the limitation of their ideas, cannot do so successfully. It is true that no prayer sent up to the Father of All shall fall fruitless to the ground, but the surmounting of the temporary difficulties of human life is not the function of the Great Unmanifest, any more than the lighting of fires is the function of the sun; yet if the rays of the sun be focussed through a burning-glass, the fire can be lighted.

The First Manifest sustains all things, and will sustain them whether we pray to It or not, and in the end we shall all be gathered back into that Infinite Life, but at the present state of our evolution It is, for all practical purposes, beyond our ken (save in certain advanced meditations when It is approached by means of a symbol) ; we are carried in the great streams of Its force like animalculæ in the tides of the sea, borne in a movement so vast that our senses cannot cognise it. It will function whether we worship It or not, and no prayer of ours can turn It a hairsbreadth from Its course.

The Cosmic Christ is a world-force ; by aspiration we can open our consciousness to it, and align ourselves with its lines of power until consciousness is suffused by it and illumination occurs; but it is not a force which relieves small human needs, though we can draw upon it for any cosmic task upon which we may be engaged. It is the Guardian of the Soul, whether we call him Saint or Master, who stretches the hand in the dark that the struggling heart demands, bringing to him the power of the Christ that, were it applied to his naked soul, would burn it ; or shielding him from that ineffable glory when it becomes so bright that the newly-opened eyes of the soul are seared by it. For the power of the Christ is so strong in its purificatory force that it is only gold which has been tried by the furnace that can stand it; all that is dross in our nature goes up in flames when exposed to its regenerative fires, and it is the function of the Guardians of Souls to temper the wind to the shorn lamb and the fiery light to the imperfect spirit, leading gently those who have conceived the Divine Ideal until such time as it shall be brought to realisation and fulfilment.

When in need of power for cosmic purposes we align consciousness with the forces of the Cosmic Christ by means of certain meditations; but when in need of comfort we reach out hands of faith through the darkness of the Veil, and from behind the Veil we feel them taken by the answering hand of the Guardian of the Soul. Silently in the night the hands may be lifted above the head and the answering grip imaged in the imagination, and then it may be found that imagination has been transformed into reality and a sudden power has touched the soul, an unseen Presence has been sensed in the darkness, and the wanderer knows that he is not alone.

CHAPTER VI

THE TRAINING AND WORK OF AN INITIATE

THOSE who seek knowledge upon the occult path win through finally to the service of a Master, and a description of the stages by which that apprenticeship is obtained will assist realisation.

All manifested life is advancing towards perfection in the great current of evolution, broad, slow, but certain; each organised unit of evolution, or group-soul of a species, is overshadowed by a great angelic consciousness that acts as individuality to the slowly evolving group-mind. When individualisation takes place within the group consciousness, each unit thus created becomes its own master and learns by bitter experience the right use of its powers, generating much karma in the process, and the group-soul of the whole, metaphorically speaking, throws its weight so as to counterbalance the composite karma thus generated, thus maintaining the racial poise ; should the over-balance proceed beyond the power of righting, the group angel, or higher soul, withdraws, and the death of the group takes place as does the death of any other body from which the soul is withdrawn.

Should the individual consciousness, thus developed, perceive the brooding spirit that overshadows the whole of which it is a part and transmits to it the Divine forces, should it conceive the idea of co-operating with the Divine Life rather than experimenting with its own personal life, then it comes out from under the dominion of the group-soul and into the jurisdiction of the Lodge of the Masters concerned with that group.

Now the Lodge of the Masters is but another name for the " body of just men made perfect," those souls which, by supreme effort, have out-distanced their fellows and attained the full stature of human development before evolutionary time has brought it about for the rest of mankind. Many souls have done this since the beginning of our race ; some, having attained completion, elect to await the end of the manvantara, or day of manifestation, in a state of beatitude ; others, however, out of compassion, return again within reach of the earth-sphere in order that they may assist those who are struggling to advance by the path which they themselves have followed. It is these that are indicated by the name of Master as generally used. There are indeed other perfected souls of the higher grades who are concerned with other work, but these should more properly be referred to as Regents ; the term Lord is usually applied to a being perfected in an earlier evolution. The Lords of Flame, Form, and Mind, however, are gradually withdrawing to more remote spheres as their work becomes stereotyped by cyclic repetition in the course of vast ages, and their tasks are taken over by the Regents, so that instead of a Lord of Form one might find oneself dealing with a Regent of the Sphere of Saturn. The distinction is an important one, especially in adjusting karma by means of astrological calculations, for the Regents are much more accessible than the Lords.

The work of an initiate, and consequently the task the aspirant has to undertake in order to prepare himself for that work, cannot be fully realised unless it be understood in connection with the process of evolution, of which it forms an integral and very vital part. The occultist believes that the work of the universe is carried on by means of a hierarchy of consciousnesses. These consciousnesses have been personified as gods, archangels or devas by different schools of belief; and although these personifications have been anthropomorphised by the unenlightened, they retain their metaphysical significance for the initiated, and the reader is asked to try and disabuse himself of the associations which uninstructed thought has allowed to gather about these entities. They differ as much in degree from the highest form of consciousness with which we are acquainted as that highest form differs from the lowest which our instruments of precision and magnification enable us to perceive; but although they differ in degree so much as hardly to be recognisable as entities to our myopic perception, they do not differ in kind from that type of organisation and activity of which our human intelligence forms one of the earlier milestones, and therefore they are better described as entities, or conscious beings, than by any other description, because such an identification with our own type of evolution serves to indicate a relationship; for what we are to-day they were in the yesterday of cosmic time, and what they are to-day we shall be in the cosmic to-morrow.

We shall understand this statement better, and realise that it is not a wild phantasy of the transcendental imagination, if we remind ourselves of the established and accepted teaching of biology concerning the evolution of man from primitive forms of life. Biology has demonstrated beyond cavil the line of the ascent of man, and the concept of a super-humanity and an archangelic kingdom is but a further continuation of that line beyond the point at which humanity now stands.

Occult science differs from orthodox science in that it looks upon man as occupying an intermediate stage on the ladder of life, instead of its topmost rung, and upon this hypothesis bases its doctrine of initiation and the speeding-up of individual evolution thereby. When it is remembered that, as can be proved historically, the mystery schools taught the doctrine of evolution at a time when orthodox science taught that of special creation and a static universe, it does not seem impossible that orthodox science may ultimately admit the rest of the esoteric hypothesis of which it has already admitted so much.

The Logoidal Consciousness is conceived of as formulating ideas concerning Its universe; these ideas are realised as spiritual ideals by the great Star Logoi, or Ray Chohans, to use the Eastern terminology; these ideals are intellectualised as abstract ideas by the Greater Masters, and are thereby brought down into manifestation as far as the plane of the Abstract Mind. Beyond this plane, the life of form begins, and for ideals to be brought through into the planes of form they have to be " formulated " by consciousnesses working in terms of form. It is at this point that the work of the Adept begins, for he, still living upon the plane of form but able to raise consciousness to the plane of the abstract mind, is able to get into rapport with the Masters and receive from Them the inspiration of the abstract ideals which it is to be his function to bring through to the plane of matter.

It will therefore be realised that the Adept acts as intermediary between the Masters and humanity; he is, in fact, one of the links in the chain whereby the Archetypal Ideas conceived in the Logoidal Consciousness are brought through into manifestation in matter.

The Adept is not, however, the last link whereby the chain of evolutionary inspiration is connected with the plane of matter, for he of necessity lives apart from the world of men because he has to maintain a footing in two worlds, and this he cannot do if he be deeply immersed in matter. Below him come his pupils, or apprentices, as they are technically termed in the Mysteries, and to these he hands on the Archetypal Ideas, duly formulated, in order that they may be *lived* out on the plane of matter and so brought through into manifestation in human consciousness. Once this has been accomplished, and the Archetypal Idea injected into the group-mind of the race by being realised and lived by a consciousness forming part of that group-mind, it is caught up by the race and forms part of its sub-consciousness, gradually permeating it, destroying ideas which are antagonistic to it and coalescing with ideas which are sympathetic, thereby changing the whole tone of the group-mind of the race. We say race advisedly, for the whole scheme is racial, being worked out through group-minds, and the racial factor cannot be ignored in any question of occult work or initiation. This does not mean that there need necessarily be racial antagonism, but there must always be racial differences until such time as evolution shall have brought humanity beyond the plane of form, and as long as those differences exist they must be allowed for in practical occultism.

The pupil of the Adept, as has already been noted, is known in the language of the Mysteries as an apprentice, and this word more truly expresses his status and relationship to his Teacher than does the more commonly used denomination of pupil ; for the term pupil implies one whose attitude towards his teacher is purely receptive, who is being educated solely for his own benefit by a teacher who has no other purpose to serve than that of education ; but the term apprentice implies a different type of relationship, for although the apprentice is indeed taught, he learns by sharing in the work of his master, thus catching " Hints of the proper craft, tricks of the tool's true play." He takes his part in the work that is going forward in his master's workshop ; his labour is essential to the scheme of operations ; he is not a mere onlooker, nor does he perform certain actions simply for the sake of acquiring manual dexterity ; the clay which he has worked to the proper consistency is not tossed back into the mass but placed by the master upon the wheel ; during the earlier stages of his training he performs the manual tasks of unskilled labour for his master ; he is used as " a hewer of wood and a drawer of water," and by these services he pays his footing in the workshop and earns the right to pick up his craft by watching the skilled craftsmen at their work. Long before the end of his apprentice-ship he will have learnt his trade, but he still has to continue to serve his master for a time, and the value of this unremunerated work again helps to pay for his training, until finally, being " out of his time," he is himself a master-craftsman, and as such has the freedom of the city.

The experience of the pupil accepted by the Masters is exactly analogous ; he serves Them in order that he may learn, and his labour is also utilised in the actual performance of the tasks upon which They are engaged. Even while he is receiving the preliminary instruction, he has to serve in Their Workshop of daily life, and it is in accordance with the way in which these humble offices are fulfilled during the probationary period that the final decision of acceptance or rejection is made. All the time the pupil is learning he is working, and as he works he learns. It is one of the tests of a true initiator that he never demands a fee, but always makes the pupil work for his training—makes him serve his time in the traditional way.

We may also conceive of the evolution of humanity as a vast army, toiling slowly along its line of march in a great column ; and, scouting far ahead of the main body, solitary outriders, swift-mounted, light-armed and without baggage, exploring the way for the rest ; spiritual guerillas, whom Paul referred to as those born out of due season. From time to time we shall see some swift-footed soul draw ahead of the great army of mankind and push on alone into the wilderness. For a period his path is solitary, but presently he catches up with the far-flung line of the scouts, and if able to give the pass-word that proves him to be of their body, is given his place in the ranks of that adventurous company, a boundary-rider of evolution, alone on his patrol, yet not out of touch with his comrades, for there are signalling-points along the line, and at certain seasons all gather in to the council.

There are certain times and places where the council is held, according to the degree being worked. The supreme council of the Great White Lodge is held beyond the planes of form and is therefore placeless, but the Star Lodges of the Rays have each their *point d'appui* on the physical plane, whether it be in the Himalayas, Mecca, Jerusalem, or its English equivalent ; this holy place is used as a focussing-point to enable those who are still on the plane of matter to get their bearings. Those on the planes beyond form are able, if need be, to descend as far as the Upper Astral, and those who can free their consciousness from the brain and rise thereto can meet them there if they be summoned. Sometimes the pilgrimage to the holy place is made in the flesh, but more often in the astral body ; sometimes it is the conscious projection of that body by the trained occultist ; sometimes the aspirant is taken thither by his Master and retains the memory as a dream ; but in all cases none returns as he went, for he has met the Great Light face to face and its glory remains upon his countenance. The uninitiated never profane the holy places on these occasions, an unseen power keeps them off ; even the very cattle are withdrawn, and whether it be pagan mount or Christian pool, in absolute stillness the great vibrations begin to throb till the place is humming like a bell ; a strange heat beats up from the ground even in mid-winter ; the astral fire glows till every object is rimmed with light ; incense, swung in no mortal censer, is heavy on the air, and a sense of innumerable presences, rank on rank, press in on every side, performing the great astral ritual that links spirit with matter ; and, under all, the roaring nature-forces can be heard like a river in flood, for it is on the high tide of the world of form that we pass out to the world of force.

To the aspirant the memory of such a visit shines out like a star in the dark night of the soul ; he who, having set his hand to the plough, turns not back when the toil in the darkness begins, but works on, awaiting the dawn, may suddenly find himself caught up in dream to meet the Master face to face and then returned to the plough-tail again with that glorious memory to comfort him, so that he may say with another seer who had the gift of song,

" Yea, though Thou then shouldst strike him from his glory,
    Blind and tormented, maddened and alone,
Even on the Cross would he maintain his story,
    Yes, and in Hell would whisper, 'I have known '."

It is the seeker who remembers in Hell what was shown him on the Mount who attains to illumination.

CHAPTER VII

THE OCCULT SCHOOLS

The training of a student of Occult Science falls into well-marked stages, whatever Ray or tradition he may be working upon. Each stage is, or should be, the preparation for the one above it, and serious harm is done when students pass from stage to stage insufficiently prepared. The conditions which are described here must not be taken as referring to any one special order or fraternity, but as being generalisations and a counsel of perfection. Fraternities have their rise and fall, as do other institutes of learning. Upon the mundane plane it is impossible to escape from the limitations of human personalities. A great occultist will make a great occult school, but upon his death the mantle may fall upon unworthy shoulders and the glory be departed or turned to corruption. The way of initiation has been rendered tortuous in the Western hemisphere by persecution and materialism, but the cloud seems to be lifting under the great impulse of spiritual power which all sensitive souls know to be flowing out upon the world at the present time ; occult orders and study groups are springing up in every direction, and it is well for the aspirant to have some idea as to what an occult school ought to be in order that he may understand whether the one in which he contemplates enrolling himself meets with the requirements of a genuine initiatory standard.

After the Reformation set men free to speculate in religious matters and worship each at his own discretion, there sprang up a rank crop of sects, some of which differed from orthodoxy in such minute details that the smallest display of tolerance and goodwill could have saved a schism; others were so wild in their doctrines and practice as to be obviously the product of disordered minds. So it is with modern occultism : a very little knowledge and some experience of the Unseen will enable a man to set up as a teacher of occultism and even an initiator ; this esoteric quackery is as remote from the spirit of the great Schools of the Mysteries as the methods of a patent medicine seller at a country fair from those of scientific therapeutics.

The great Mystery Schools have existed from the dawn of consciousness in the human race ; they are neither fabrications of the imagination, frauds to dupe the superstitious, nor existent solely on the Inner Planes. Outside Europe they have flourished unchecked from time immemorial, revered and feared by the peoples they guided ; sometimes fallen upon evil days, as the degenerate voodoo schools of the negro, sometimes retaining a noble tradition, as in certain of the Indian and Chinese schools, but always accepted as a part of the racial life just as are the monastic orders among ourselves.

In Europe, however, the state religion, which should have been the custodian of the Mysteries, became instead their persecutor. This unhappy state of affairs came about owing to the political expediency which placed men in high positions who did not hold high degrees in the Mysteries.

These men, such being human nature, were naturally disinclined to defer to their inferiors in office who were their superiors in knowledge, and so the esoteric teachings, which should have formed the inner school of the Church, became interdict as heresies.

Before the Reformation systematic persecution effectually stamped out all attempts at a Gnosis ; and after the Reformation the unguided intellect of the age, reacting against the doctrines of an unilluminated theology, despised all transcendentalism as superstition. Occult pursuits were therefore limited either to the very few who in any age are capable of independent thought, or the very ignorant among whom a traditional magic still survived the civilising influences of the time, such as they were. These latter brought a discredit upon the science of the Unseen that forced its worthier students to conceal their interest, and therefore Occult Science in Europe led for several centuries a hunted life, and developed the defects that such an existence must invariably give rise to.

The Archetypal Concepts, however, remained on the Inner Planes, and whenever individual men were able to raise consciousness thereto they found that the great Inner Orders still existed in the Unseen, though persecution had destroyed their physical forms. It was as if the immortal spirit of the Mysteries survived the death of its physical body— the Temple—and those who were able to raise consciousness to a higher plane could communicate with the dead Orders.

During the last half-century innumerable attempts have been made to induce the soul of the Mysteries to reincarnate, and these attempts have met with

varying success. Out of many abortive efforts a
tradition is gradually being re-formed; the smoulder-
ing fire of occult knowledge has been fanned to a
blaze, and the gods have again drawn near to man.

During the Dark Ages of European occultism any
form of Lodge work was almost impossible, for the
gathering together of a number of persons was
difficult to conceal, and roused suspicion. The
apprenticeship system of training was therefore
used by the few European initiates who kept the
spark alive. They took individual pupils into their
laboratories, just as a master craftsman did into his
workshop; and these pupils, after the death of the
Adept, usually either scattered for the purpose of
seeking further instruction, or took pupils on their
own account if sufficiently advanced. The draw-
backs of this system can readily be seen; like all
unsupervised teaching, it tended to slackness and
degeneration, and for this reason the Western
Esoteric Tradition on the physical plane does not
possess a great literature like the Eastern Tradition.
Nevertheless, as no student of the subject needs to
be reminded, the most important part of an Order is
on the Inner Planes, and these Inner Orders remained
intact down through the ages, receiving the rare
initiates who were able to find their way to them
through pure intuition, and biding their time till
men should once again be free to build the temple
that should hold the shrine.

When a temple has been thus builded, and the
altar orientated according to the best knowledge of
the artificers, it is necessary to light the Sacred
Fire. This can only be done by bringing a live
coal from another altar, unless the High Priest
is of the Order of Prometheus—and there are not

many such. Or, to vary the metaphor, apostolic succession is of the essence of initiation for the reason that the teacher has to induce in the soul of his pupil a particular type of activity, and unless he himself be functioning in this way he is unable to do so. He has to cause the higher consciousness of his pupil, hitherto lying dormant, to start functioning. This is done by means of the process known as the sympathetic induction of vibration.

If a piano and a harp are standing near each other, and a certain note be struck on the piano, the corresponding note will sound forth on the harp because the vibrations of the air, proceeding from the vibrating piano cord, impinge upon the harp strings, and the one of them that is capable of vibrating to that rhythm is set in motion. So it is with the initiator and his pupil. The activity of the higher self of the initiator stimulates that of the pupil. This is the most vital part of an occult training. The theory of occultism can be learned from books that are now available for the general public, but it is only from the functioning occultist that a student can receive the spiritual inoculation which shall work in his veins. Very few souls have ever been able to conceive by the Holy Ghost, and the study of books on embryology will not bring them much nearer to their goal.

The Priests of the Order of Prometheus are those Light-Bearers who institute the new degrees in the Mysteries as the advance of evolution renders man able to receive further teaching. They are the first bestowers of a degree that has not hitherto been worked upon the earth. It must not be thought, however, that when a man comes forward with a new teaching he is necessarily a Priest of the Order of Prometheus. The Order of Prometheus is the next highest degree to the Order of Melchisedec, and these degrees are not conferred upon the simple and ignorant as are the mystic degrees of the Inner Light, such as the Quakers know, but represent the higher spiritual attainments of an initiate. It will be remembered that Moses was taken as an infant into the palace of the Pharaohs and that the Lord Jesus was "taken into Egypt" as a young child. The significance of these words will need no emphasis to the student of esoteric science. Beware of the self-taught occultist; he is as unreliable as the self-taught healer.

Great weight is attached to apostolic succession, or derivation from a genuine tradition; no occult work, as distinguished from mystic development, is possible without it. It may be that the coal that is brought to the newly-consecrated altar is to all outward view a very dead cinder indeed, but if there be the least spark of fire within, it can be blown to a flame, and then a judicious accumulation of fuel will enable the true altar fire to blaze up and initiations to be performed by its light and heat. For the altar fire two things are necessary: the live coal, and a supply of fuel; although the apostolic succession be brought from a genuine tradition, unless there be occult knowledge, unless the temple be properly orientated, the fire cannot be blown to flame; and even after it has been duly kindled and builded, it may still be allowed to go out through lack of fuel or choking ash. Not everyone that cries "Lord Lord," is called of our Father.

An occult school can only be founded by an initiate of one of the great traditions. It will be recalled that Paracelsus travelled in the Near East before he received occult power; it will also be remembered that Mme. Blavatsky penetrated into Tibet before she was able to establish an esoteric school. The reason that the Lesser Mysteries of Europe use the terminology of the building trade is that the necessary contacts for the degrees were found in the debased rituals that the mediæval building guilds performed " for luck " when laying foundation stones. These rituals dated back to the times when temples of the Mysteries were designed as great symbols and systems of correspondences, and the men who did the work had therefore to be initiated into certain lower degrees in order that they might adequately perform their tasks. Only initiate workmen could be allowed to build these symbolic temples, just as only initiate caretakers can look after Masonic temples, and so an elementary knowledge of the Mysteries was as much a part of the training of the better type of builder as an elementary knowledge of mechanics.

When temple-building gave place to church-building, the tradition survived for a long time. The builders persisted in raising their structures due east and west and working into them a mass of ancient symbolism that their new employers failed to recognise as anything more than ornament. Not that the operative masons had any such esoteric designs as are attributed to them by imaginative writers, for they were seldom initiates of the Greater Mysteries, but they were possessed of stock patterns and lacked original ideas, and thus many of the symbols of ancient faiths have been preserved for us in our Christian buildings long after all shadow of knowledge had been lost to the men who wrought

them. The old rituals were retained as superstitious luck-bringers after the manner of the child
who prayed regularly, " Lead us not into Thames
Station," but when men of knowledge in 1717
wanted living fire for their newly-raised altar, they
found that the ancient rituals yielded a few live
coals under all their smother of ash, and availed
themselves of them.

CHAPTER VIII

THERE are two Paths to the Innermost: the Way of the Mystic, which is the way of devotion and meditation, a solitary and subjective path; and the way of the occultist, which is the way of the intellect, of concentration, and of the trained will; upon this path the co-operation of fellow workers is required, firstly for the exchange of knowledge, and secondly because ritual magic plays an important part in this work, and for this the assistance of several is needed in most of the greater operations. The mystic derives his knowledge through the direct communion of his higher self with the Higher Powers; to him the wisdom of the occultist is foolishness, for his mind does not work in that way; but, on the other hand, to a more intellectual and extrovert type, the method of the mystic is impossible until long training has enabled him to transcend the planes of form. We must therefore recognise these two distinct types among those who seek the Way of Initiation, and remember that there is a path for each.

The occultist goes by a well-marked way which has been trodden by countless feet from time immemorial. As soon as he has reached a certain stage of inner development, the Mystery Schools of his race are open to him, and to these he finds his way by a method which will be described in detail in a later chapter. The origin of these Mystery Schools and the source of their knowledge has been described in an earlier chapter, and in these pages we will undertake the task of explaining something of their general discipline and organisation, the reader being again reminded that these descriptions must not be taken as referring to any particular school, but as generalisations.

Esoteric science begins where exoteric science ends. The latter derives its knowledge from observation of phenomena ; the former works by intuitive methods. It is exceedingly desirable that all knowledge should be of that exact nature which only observation and experiment can produce, but the orthodox scientific method is a slow process, and meanwhile man had to live his life and cope with his environment, and therefore, in order to understand himself and solve his problems, availed himself of every faculty of the mind, including the faculty of intuition or subconscious mentation, and also of direct apprehension. Details of these two methods of mentation are too lengthy to be entered upon now, and properly form part of the subject-matter of esoteric psychology.

Exoteric science may be conceived as raising a noble and permanent dome in stone, and esoteric science as being the timber scaffolding that holds the unfinished walls in place until such time as the keystone is finally dropped into position. As each fresh course of masonry goes in, the timber comes out, for it is no longer needed; and as each new discovery adds to the domain of exact scientific knowledge, esoteric science withdraws further into the Unseen, still serving its purpose of a temporary framework that enables men's minds to operate and life to be carried on in a purposive fashion.   It is x, the unknown quantity of our mundane algebra, which enables the calculation to be worked ; but the problem cannot be regarded as finally solved until x itself is reduced to a numerical quantity and ceases to be unknown.

So it is with esoteric science ; the day will finally come when the rising tide of human consciousness, advancing with evolution, will cover all the sands of the desert, and there will be no esoteric science left, because all has become exoteric ; but that day is not yet, nor is the glow of its dawn yet visible from even the highest mountain-peak of hope, and we must therefore be content to work with x, our unknown quantity, by means of mental processes which are not applicable in the laboratory of the scientist.

The great esoteric Orders are in possession of detailed cosmogonies concerning the Unseen Worlds which press about that little of manifestation which is perceived by the five physical senses, and just as the telescope and microscope opened up to man's knowledge whole universes of new life which were imperceptible to the unaided senses, so do certain little-known powers of the mind, when these are developed, reveal plane beyond plane of existence unsuspected by the average man.   The esoteric schools teach the use of these powers because they are to the occultist what the microscope is to the biologist, and by their use he is able to acquaint himself with those states of existence which elude the human mind in its present stage of development.

The student, however, is not equipped with these powers and turned out into the Unknown to experiment as best he may, as is the research worker in natural science, but is instructed to use his newly-awakened faculties to acquaint himself at first-hand with a cosmogony which is already well known to him in theory. The difference between these two methods is the difference between the sailing of Columbus for America and the sailing of a modern liner ; the captain of the latter has his charts and navigating instruments and can tell exactly where he is at any given moment and make the landfall of any place upon the long line of the Atlantic seaboard by night or by day without having to grope for it ; whereas Columbus depended entirely upon luck to make his landfall, and it was only the fact that it was physically impossible for him to pass America without seeing it that prevented him from doing so. When it is recalled that Columbus was really trying to get to India and believed that he had done so, it will be realised that the position of natural science may not be quite as satisfactory as is sometimes supposed. True, it has found much dry land, but is that dry land the India it believes it to be ?

It is the possession of map and compasses that distinguishes the initiate of a true occult Order from the natural psychic who is groping his way out into the Unseen by rule of thumb. The map is a cosmogony and System of Correspondences which enables the student to find his way up and down the planes of the Unseen ; with this chart he knows the roads ; without it he must struggle cross-country as best he may.

A System of Correspondences consists of a set of symbols which the concrete mind can apprehend and a knowledge of the association chains which connect them with each other; this knowledge is absolutely essential for occult development, and it is different for each of the great main divisions of mankind and of the earth's surface because local conditions vary, and upon its astral and mundane aspects the system has to be adapted to them, although in its higher aspects it is universal. For instance, many occult operations are best performed at a certain time; and time is different in different longitudes; therefore the operation which should be performed at a certain hour in London would have to be performed five hours later in New York; for it may not depend upon sun-time, but upon sidereal time, and that is constant for the whole globe; and the difference in sun-time between one part and another has to be allowed for. Likewise, in any process which has relation to magnetic currents and tides, these have to be calculated for the spot where the operation is to occur, and cannot be set going at random. All these considerations will show that practical occultism is not a thing to be learnt out of books by the uninitiated. An Order knows the methods of raising and developing consciousness best suited to the land and race to which it belongs, and without such guidance a student of the Secret Science is at a grave disadvantage.

In order to avail oneself of the chart, however, it is necessary to have navigating instruments and understand their use, otherwise one might know where America was, but be quite ignorant of one's own whereabouts in relation to it. The instruments of the occultist are certain little-known faculties of the mind, trained and developed by certain definite processes. Not much can be said in these pages concerning the work of the Greater Mysteries which is carried on by the Orders, but enough has been said to make it clear that they possess the secret cosmogony and understand the methods of training the higher consciousness.

Before such a training can be undertaken, however, it is necessary that the lower consciousness and character should receive a thorough purification and discipline, so that foundations are laid deep and sure that will not shift or yield when the great superstructure of occult knowledge is raised upon them through the functioning of the higher mind.   Unless this be done, disaster is very likely to occur ; in fact, one might say that it is certain to occur.   Many souls, of course, have received initiation in previous lives, and therefore soon recapitulate and recall their old knowledge when they come in touch with the Mysteries again, but even for these it is well to rub up their past memories and be sure that they have brought them through into waking consciousness in their entirety before undertaking the perilous task of occult development ; but for the soul that is coming on to the Path for the first time, such a preliminary training is absolutely essential.   A very large proportion of the disasters that occur in the pursuit of practical occultism are due to the neglect of the preliminary training, so that the foundations could not carry the superstructure.   An occult school is a gymnasium of the mind, and if a student attempts to do certain feats when he is untrained or out of condition, a serious accident may occur and he may be injured for life, whereas, when he is properly trained he can perform the same feat with perfect safety.   The exercises that develop the higher consciousness have to be graduated just as carefully as those that develop the body, and ignorance or a faulty system produce just as bad results in the Lodge as in the gymnasium. It is a maxim among athletes that no man can train himself, and this is just as true among occultists, as a good many adventurous students have found to their cost. Occultism is a great adventure, and it is not without its risks, though, under proper conditions, these risks are such as a brave man may not consider himself unjustified in taking. It is not unlike mountaineering in this respect: there is always a certain element of danger, and that element may unexpectedly assume serious proportions which no man can foresee; but given good guides, good ropes, and a steady head, there is no reason why a man should not habituate himself to the heights by attempting the easier climbs, and finally be able to conquer the classic peaks of mountaineering. But the man who comes straight out of a London office, and without guides, maps, ropes, or anything but an out-of-date Baedeker, sets out to walk up the Matterhorn, would either get no further than the next village or come to an untimely end.

The preliminary training which fits a man for the heights of occult science is, or ought to be, given in that section of the Mysteries which is known as the Fraternities. It is the function of the Fraternities to train the personality of the pupil, and in the process to weed out those who are unfit for the heights in the present incarnation. No one need be ashamed, after having won into a Fraternity, to be unable to go any further; we all have to spend several incarnations working in the Lesser Mysteries before we are ready for the Greater Mysteries, and although when one has succeeded in setting foot on the first rung of the ladder the way lies open to him, it must not be thought that it is possible to climb to the top of the ladder in a single incarnation. Those who make phenomenally rapid progress are recapitulating that which they have done in past lives, and those who make slow progress are working up the Mysteries for the first time ; there is nothing to be ashamed of in this slow progress if one is honestly doing one's best, and the time is not wasted, but essential to the training ; but one has to be very wary of attempting to travel at the pace that is only possible in a recapitulation, or disaster will ensue.

In a Fraternity the training of character is especially stressed, and the great lessons of brotherhood and selfless service have to be learned. The conscious mind has also to be got ready for its amalgamation with super-consciousness, and for this purpose it has to be equipped with the general theory of occult science. In the Lesser Mysteries, therefore, the aspirant trains his character as an athlete trains his body in order that it may be strengthened to stand the ordeal of the heights to which the Greater Mysteries will enable him to climb. He also seeks to equip his mind so that he may fully understand the teaching that will be conveyed to him when he enters the Greater Mysteries.

Much of the teaching received in the Lesser Mysteries is not now secret but is available in many modern publications ; nevertheless, its concepts have to be thoroughly grasped before the student is a fit candidate for the Greater Mysteries, where its real significance is revealed. It is, however, in the character-training that the value of the Lesser Mysteries chiefly lies, and in the fact that the member of a Fraternity is under the influence of one or another of the great Orders ; for a Fraternity, to be able to give a valid training, must be the pendant of one of the great initiation traditions, and unless an initiate of the Greater Mysteries occupy the East, its ceremonies will be invalid.

Finally, we come to the consideration of the function of the group or society in the study of the Sacred Science. Such groups are innumerable at the present time, and may either represent the door ajar, or be a snare and a delusion, or even something worse. The methods of discriminating between the worthy and the unworthy are given in detail in a later chapter.

A group or society is nothing more than a study circle unless its leader is an initiate of the Mysteries, for a group should be the pendant of a Fraternity, just as a Fraternity is the pendant of an Order. Initiates of the Mysteries who have arrived at a certain degree are permitted to work openly in the world, teaching the elements of occult science to all who will listen, but no more than the elements can be given out thus freely for reasons that have already been considered. Such a lecturer or writer does little more than act as a signpost ; he says to his students, " If you follow the line of preparation which I indicate, you will be able to qualify for occult training." This, also, is all that the propaganda societies are able to do in their public lectures, but it goes without saying that it is an absolutely necessary task and must be done by somebody, and the initiates of the Mysteries are required to serve their time in this work.

If the leader of a group or the president of a society be indeed an initiate of the Mysteries, he

will pass his students on to an inner school where
they will receive further training, and thus he will
be able to set their feet upon the path ; but if he
be not himself a regular initiate, in touch with one
of the great systems, he will have nothing to offer
his students beyond the resources of his own intellect, and that is a fountain which the more advanced
among them will soon drink dry.

The groups and societies should be looked upon
as the outposts of the Mysteries, and it is the aim
of every true teacher to pass his pupils through his
hands as speedily as may be and send them on to
the Order where he himself received his training.
The quicker he can bring them to the state of
development required for admission to the Mysteries
the greater his skill as a teacher. The man who is
an initiate of one of the great Mystery Schools never
fears to let his pupils outdistance him, because he
knows that it stands him in good stead with his
superiors if he is constantly sending up to them
aspirants who " make good." He therefore never
tries to hold back a promising pupil, because he has
no need to fear that that pupil, if allowed to penetrate into the Mysteries, would spy out the naked-
ness of the land ; he will rather bring back a report
of its exceeding richness, and thereby confirm the
statements of his teacher and spur his fellow-pupils
to yet greater eagerness.

Never trust the occultist who tells you that he is
the head of a tradition, because if he were, in the
first place, he would not tell the fact to the uninitiated, and in the second place he would in all
probability be living in great seclusion and inacces-
sible to all but his immediate subordinates. If a
man is a great artist he does not need to inform us

of the fact; we shall know him by his pictures that are hung in the galleries of the nation, and we shall, moreover, find that he guards himself from casual acquaintances because of the inroads on his time to which his fame renders him liable. The more eminent a person, the harder he is to approach, not out of any spirit of pride and exclusiveness, but because so many people want to see him that discrimination has to be used in admitting them.

So it is with the occultist—the great ones are not easy to find, and the ones that are accessible are either among the smaller fry, or are Guides to bring the seeker to the Mystery School where they themselves received their training. The genuine occultist does not make his secrets up out of his head, but receives them as a great and sacred responsibility, given to him by men who themselves have received them from their predecessors; and so the torch of occult knowledge is handed on down the generations.

This, then, is the organisation of the occult schools: first, the groups that gather about initiates of the Lesser Mysteries; then the Fraternity that is a pendant of the Greater Mysteries; and finally the Greater Mysteries, the Order itself, wherein the real occult work begins. It is up this ladder that the aspirant climbs towards the light, and his progress depends on none but himself, for even the Order upon this earth is but the gateway that leads into the Unseen; it is from the Great Initiator alone that he can take his initiation, and that initiation is not given in the flesh or by the flesh. Groups, Orders and Fraternities work in symbols, and in them he sees as in a glass darkly; but it is their function to help him to develop super-consciousness, and when he has achieved it he shall see face to face and know even as he is known.

It must again be emphasised that the study of occultism is only a means to an end, and that end is the Way of Divine Union. Some there are who can take that journey direct, but others have to proceed by stages through the planes of form, of which the mental plane is not the least, and for them the mind has to be trained and raised and taught to function under new forms that shall more nearly approximate to the spiritual actuality. But let it never be forgotten that all forms but obscure the light, and we only know them by the shadows they throw upon a lower plane. The aspirant should use the symbols of occultism to train consciousness, not to furnish it, and it should be his aim to cast them aside at the earliest possible moment that pure consciousness can dawn upon him.

CHAPTER IX

THE Inner Light alone can bring a man to the Great
Light ; but this is a supreme achievement, and to
correlate such an experience with normal consciousness, so that it shall not pass like a flash of lightning,
it is necessary that consciousness should be prepared
for its reception. When it be remembered that each
object upon the plane of physical form has within
it substance of each of the other six planes of manifestation, and each aspect of substance is shaped
into a form according to the laws and types of its
own plane, it will be seen that every material object
has analogies upon every plane of the manifested
universe. It is by the use of these analogies that
systems of symbolism are built up.

  If those who have knowledge of the Divine Light
in any of its aspects wish to assist a neophyte to
obtain a conscious realisation of the nature of that
Light, they have to supply him with a chain of
associated ideas, a veritable Jacob's ladder, leading
right up the planes with an accurate correlation
upon each. Not every object which may be chosen
at random according to superficial resemblance to
the thing intended to symbolise can do this, and only
those who themselves can lift consciousness plane
by plane are competent to work out a system of
symbology, and of such, those who can pass through

the seven planes are very rare; therefore it is that
initiators of a lesser calibre are content to rely upon
the symbolism of the Manus of their race even if
they themselves are unable to interpret its higher
aspects, because they know that their pupil, when
he achieves to the plane on which he is entitled to
receive any degree of initiation, will be able, having
once been shown the mundane symbol, to make that
interpretation for himself. It is therefore of great
value to have access to the ancient rituals which the
Great Ones of the past designed, Manu, Saviour and
Master, working each in His degree.

Every object in a Lodge should be a symbolic
representation of the different aspects of force
functioning upon the plane to which it is intended
to raise the consciousness of the candidate. Nothing
should be omitted, and nothing extraneous included. The creation in consciousness of an image
of the symbol forms a point of contact with the
force it is intended to represent. Form, colour,
movement, sound, and incense make their appeal to
the gates of the physical senses, each of which is an
analogue of the subtle senses, and thus the symbolic image is built up which, provided that conditions are right, will be translated into experience
by the subtle body upon which it is designed to act.

It has been well and truly said that in the exoteric
church the ceremony is performed by one person
for the benefit of the congregation; but in the
Lodge the ceremony is performed by the congregation for the benefit of one person. The candidate
is the principal actor in a mystery play wherein he
passes in symbolic action through certain experiences
of the soul in its passage from darkness to light. It
is intended thereby to recall to memory experiences

through which the soul has passed in ultra-consciousness, and unless the initiator has this basis of subconscious achievement to work upon, initiation is a meaningless ceremony to the candidate. Each degree of initiation marks the completion, not the commencement, of a stage on the Path. Let it be clearly understood that ritual initiation in the Lesser Mysteries bestows nothing, it merely renders available that which has been attained in ultra-consciousness. The real initiation is a spiritual experience. To pass through the symbolic representation of death and resurrection can mean nothing to a candidate in whom desire is not dead and spiritual consciousness has not arisen.

It is recorded of the ancient Mysteries that the candidate for initiation into the different Fraternities was usually made to act out the life-story of the original Hierophant, the Divine Man whose history formed the basis of the symbolism of the ceremonies. He took the leading part in a mystery play in which the other parts were played by the Lodge officers. The Divine Man was the archetype or ideal which was to be held in consciousness by the neophyte, and each officer of the Lodge represented a force which played upon the Divine Man in the course of his evolution. An officer who rightly understood his function would dwell upon the force which should act through his office till his personality became so saturated with it that he radiated its influence upon the candidate he was helping to initiate. The united action of all the officers builds a group-mind which is capable of transmitting and focussing potencies of a much more massive or cosmic type than could be transmitted through the channel of a single consciousness.

Colour and sound play important parts in the operation of transmuting the forces of one plane into their correspondences on a lower and denser level. Their influence has its basis in the principles of the law of the Ratio of Vibration ; this can be best explained by analogy. It is well known that many people associate colours with certain musical tones ; it is also a proven fact that if sand be scattered on a disc and a violin bow drawn across its edge, causing it to vibrate, the sand will assume regular patterns consisting of geometrical forms ; sound is a vibration of the air, of which the number of vibrations per second of any given note can be ascertained ; light is a vibration of the ether of which the number of vibrations per second of any given colour can also be ascertained, and it will be found that there is a mathematical relationship between the air-vibration of a sound and the ether-vibration of the colour which it evokes in the consciousness of certain people of the more sensitive type ; the latter will be a multiple of the former. Upon the subtler planes are many different types of force, each with its own vibration-rhythm ; if the rate of that rhythm can be discovered, and either its root or prime factors be ascertained, and sounds be formulated which have the vibration-rate of the several factors, and these be enunciated in sequence, they will evoke the complementary vibration in the subtle body which corresponds to the plane of the potency it is intended to evoke, just as the musical tone causes the colour to which it bears a ratio to rise in consciousness. This is the rationale of the use of Sacred Names and Words of Power.

And likewise with geometrical forms : certain composite influences have their correspondences in the intersecting lines of force which give rise to the regular figures of the sand patterns ; upon a similar principle are constructed the Sacred Symbols which represent lines of force in the Unseen.

All these influences are employed to construct a great thought-form in the group-mind of the Lodge, and into this thought-form are poured the potencies evoked by the Names of Power used in the initiatory work, and these influences are focussed upon the candidate while he is in a state of exalted consciousness. This is the rationale of initiation.

The candidate, while acting out the ritual with his physical body, should remember that he himself is but a symbol of the Divine Man he is made to represent, and he should follow out in consciousness the processes of the soul that are being enacted on the subtle planes.

CHAPTER X

THOSE without the gate frequently question the wisdom and right of the occultist to guard his knowledge by the imposition of oaths of secrecy. We are so accustomed to see the scientist give his beneficent discoveries freely to all mankind that we feel that humanity is wronged and defrauded if any knowledge be kept secret by its discoveries and not at once made available for all who desire to share in it.

To this charge the initiate replies that he is the guardian of this knowledge on humanity's behalf, and just as a trustee would not permit a minor to fling away his fortune in rash extravagance or foolish speculation before he was of an age to understand the nature of his responsibilities, so the Elder Brethren will not allow humanity to burn its fingers with great unknown potencies until it has reached a stage of development that shall have rendered it sufficiently wise, disciplined and purified to be trusted with them.

The knowledge is reserved in order that humanity may be protected from its abuse in the hands of the unscrupulous. Anyone who understands the nature of the Secret Science and the powers it bestows will see the need for such precaution. The mind has certain little-known powers which are so potent and so subtle that, used for crime, they could overturn

the social system of a nation.   The courts recognise
that undue influence can be exercised by one person
over another, but they have little realisation of the
kind of influence a trained mind can exert over an
untrained one.   The true initiate uses this power in
order to develop and train the higher faculties of his
pupil, but the follower of the Left-hand Path uses
it for his own ends, without regard to the interest or
welfare of those over whom he may obtain influence.
It is therefore in the interests of humanity that the
knowledge which confers such powers should be
retained in trustworthy hands, just as it is necessary
that the power to obtain powerful and dangerous
drugs should be safeguarded so that they may only
be procured for legitimate purposes by reputable
people.

The initiate of the Right-hand Path uses every
endeavour to ensure that the Secret Science shall be
taught to worthy pupils and to these alone.   For
this reason he binds each pupil he takes by an oath of
secrecy lest the neophyte should communicate the
knowledge he receives before he is in a position to
appreciate its significance.   A certain amount of
discretion is allowed to the initiates of the higher
degrees—they can loose as well as bind ; but most of
the systems of occult training are guarded by very
strict obligations, and the Adept himself is bound by
oath only to communicate them on the conditions
under which he himself has received them.   So we
see some of the old systems guarding with terrible
oaths information that has long since been printed
and published ; and it is a standing jest against one
of the great Western systems that its initiates would
bring down the powers of Hell on their heads if they
disclosed the Hebrew alphabet.   But although there

are points upon which the occult schools might with profit reconsider their position, there can be little doubt in the mind of anyone acquainted with the nature of the work undertaken in a school of practical occultism that an oath of secrecy is necessary.

No initiate of the Right-hand Path would ever withhold knowledge from anyone who was worthy to receive it ; rather does he desire to come bringing with him his sheaves when called to enter the Great White Lodge ; he seeks earnestly for pupils whom he can train to assist him in his work, for without such assistance many tasks are impossible to him. But, on the other hand, he dare not, for his own protection if for no worthier motive, accept as a pupil anyone likely to abuse that knowledge or betray that trust. For this reason he subjects his pupils to tests and only admits them gradually to the knowledge he holds, so that, should they, under the stress of occult training, reveal unsuspected flaws of character, they may be rejected before they have gone far enough to be dangerous. The critic of the Adepts would form a truer opinion of their attitude if he did not look upon them as guardians of a treasure, grudgingly doling it out to applicants whose rights it was impossible to ignore or defy, but rather as trainers of racehorses, patiently trying beast after beast in the hope that one may ultimately be found that will win the Grand National. The Adept who accepts an unsuitable pupil is guilty of cruelty just as much as the rider who sends a horse at a fence it cannot take.

But although the seeker after initiation must be prepared to accept an oath of secrecy as one of the conditions of his training, it is held in the West that

he should not be asked to accept an oath of obedience.   In the East, however, this is not the case,
and many, if not most Eastern schools, and schools
deriving from the East, demand such an oath as part
of their discipline.   They are no doubt the best
judges of the needs of the souls committed to their
care, but such a system does not suit the Western
temperament, trained for generations in freedom,
and was never a part of the Western Tradition, even
at a time when the nations it served still maintained
slavery and autocracy.   It is quite true that, for
initiation, the pupil must offer unreserved dedication
to his Master, but he should allow no one to interpret
for him the terms of that dedication; his own Higher
Self should be the sole judge.   The true initiator
will help him to find his Master, but should never for
one single moment stand between him and that
Master, and if such an attempt is made the pupil is
counselled to brush it peremptorily aside.   True, an
occultist of a higher degree may bring through to
him a message or instruction from his Master, but
he should never regard it as authoritative unless it
" causes his heart to burn within him," unless there
is that response of intuition which makes it valid for
him.

Supposing, for instance, an Adept should say to a
neophyte that the Master has given such-and-such
an instruction to him, and the neophyte replies,
" That does not seem right to me," who is to be the
judge ?   Most unquestionably the neophyte, for it
is better for his advancement that he should err as a
man than be thrust forward as a slave ; he will learn
more from an honest mistake than from an un-
intelligent reliance on the judgment of another.
Rashness and overweening self-confidence will no

doubt receive their rebuke, but the man who has the courage of his convictions is more likely to win through to initiation than the one who is content to let someone else do his thinking for him. Advice is one thing, and commands are another. Advice is given in order that it may enlighten the understanding, and is only to be followed after mature consideration ; a man of a Western race will generally reply that it is incompatible with his manhood to take orders in questions of conscience from a fallible fellow-creature. It is a bold man who will assume the responsibility of guiding another soul blindfold between Heaven and Hell.

The true trainer of souls knows that it serves no useful purpose to require such an oath, for unless he is prepared to carry his pupils bodily into the Kingdom of Heaven he must teach them to walk upon their own feet, and he can never do that as long as he keeps them in the splints of an oath of obedience. And indeed, were he so to carry them, it is very doubtful if Heaven would have them, for initiation requires great qualities of character, and these cannot be learnt save in freedom. The Mysteries always demand of a man that he shall be free as well as of good repute, and this is not a mere form of words retained from ancient times, for if a man is of such a nature that he passes readily under the domination of a fellow-being without instinctively resenting the process, he will be very liable to pass under the domination of beings who are not his fellows and fall a victim to obsession.

What is required of the neophyte is not a blind obedience but an intelligent comprehension of principles. His teacher demands of him that he shall have reached such a degree of self-discipline that, when a principle is explained to him, he will immediately be able to put it into practice without the bray of Brother Ass becoming unduly loud. For instance, if the Adept should instruct the neophyte to watch till dawn, he expects the neophyte to be able to keep himself awake, and is not going to sit up all night and prod him whenever he shows signs of nodding. How is any test to be passed if the pupil is accustomed to obey instructions instead of thinking for himself ? The tests of occultism are based partly on the intelligent application of principles to circumstances and partly on character and stamina, and a capacity for blind obedience is not going to take an aspirant through these tests.

The request for an oath of obedience does not sound well, for if obedience is required for purposes which would obtain the approval of the pupil, why should not he, as a free man, give his loyalty ? And if they are of such a nature as not to command his acceptance, is it right that he should be coerced against his conscience ? If the light that is in him be so dim that he cannot understand the principles involved, he should not be placed in the position of having to deal with problems beyond his powers. Would you make a child in the kindergarten swear loyalty to Euclid and obedience to his principles ? When he understands the propositions of Euclid he will see that they are self-evident. And so it is with occult principles : they are natural laws, not arbitrary enactments, and to argue with them is like flogging a dead donkey. If would-be teachers of occult science would realise that their position is as impregnable as that of an astronomer, and that they can safely leave a recalcitrant pupil to be dealt with by the laws he defies, there would be much less talk of schism and rebellion in occult schools. In these matters no man has any need to take the law into his own hands, whether he be pupil or initiator. Supposing the pupil of an astronomer threatened to jump off the earth, would his teacher lock him up in order to save his life ? Supposing he threatened to do an injury to the moon, would he make him swear a solemn oath to refrain ? The Masters can take care of Themselves, and if we persist in poking sticks into the cosmic wheels, it is we who get a broken wrist and no thanks for our pains.

If a teacher bases his teaching upon spiritual principles, he can safely leave his pupils to these principles, whether for reward or punishment. The man who takes his stand upon such principles is in an impregnable position and nothing can dislodge him, Even if he be a neophyte groping in darkness, spiritual principle is the thread that will take him through the labyrinth ; if he releases his hold upon it he is lost ; if he maintains it he can be his own initiator. One of the tests of the Mysteries tempts the aspirant to an unprincipled act in the name of the Masters, and if he have so little under-standing of Their nature as to yield, he is rejected.

" Thou shalt love the Lord thy God with all thy heart and with all thy soul and with all thy strength," and " *Him only* shalt thou serve " ; the function of teacher, initiator, fraternity, or order, is to bring you to God, not to take the place of God and demand your loyalty. " Only follow me so far as I follow the Masters," said H. P. B., and she spoke as a true initiator. All white occultists tell you never to surrender your will ; they should also tell you never to surrender your judgment. The teacher who asks you to follow blindly is no more training you than a mathematician who uses the same method. If a suggestion does not appeal to your reason and conscience, reject it. Those who climb high are subject to great temptations, and we never know when the vertigo of the heights may seize even the greatest ; there are matters in which onlookers often see most of the game, and the wayfaring man, though a fool, may sometimes form a clearer judgment than those whose eyes are blinded by too much light.

Questions of principle have nothing to do with the intellect, they concern character ; and however little you may know of occultism, you are competent to decide a question of principle by the guidance of your conscience, which, for you, is the voice of the Master.

CHAPTER XI

THE distinction between White and Black occultism is not as easy to draw as the naïve and inexperienced would like to believe. In order to understand it, it is necessary to define the esoteric concept of evil.

If we compare the teaching of the Old and New Testament we shall find that under the Old Dispensation life was regulated by innumerable minutely detailed regulations which told a man exactly what to do in any given circumstances. These regulations, being detailed and precise, were inelastic, and, as conditions of social life changed, became inapplicable; they gave no instructions concerning matters that greatly needed regulation, and obsolete laws remained as irksome and needless restrictions. For the interpretation and application of the Mosaic Law were developed hosts of scribes and commentators who by the exercise of great ingenuity and much stretching of the meaning of words, succeeded in maintaining them as a more or less workable system. When the Master Jesus came, however, He said: "Behold a new commandment give I unto you," and in some two dozen words He gave the principles underlying the Law and the Prophets. He said: "Thou shalt love the Lord thy God with all thy heart and with all thy soul and with all thy mind and with all thy strength . . . and thy neighbour as thyself."—This is a comprehensive statement which sophistry cannot elude and which can serve as a guide in all imaginable circumstances. It is a measuring-rod which, upon whatever plane we may be functioning, will always give true measure. We can apply it to our dealings with elementals as well as men, with the loftiest intelligences and the most debased of evil spirits. It is a rule of conduct which never fails us.

In estimating external conditions, however, we need some further guidance, and herein it is impossible to apply a standard ruling ; a thing which may be right under one circumstance may be wrong under another ; a thing which may be right for one person may be wrong for another ; there is no Levitical Code which can be applied to the infinite variety of the tests on the Path.

The initiate takes as standard, not an ethical foot-rule, but movement and direction. He measures all things against the current of evolution. He asks of any given action or set of circumstances : Is it moving in the same direction as evolution, and is its pace faster or slower than the normal tide ? And he will judge relative rightness or wrongness by the answers to these two questions.

For instance, he might consider the work and teachings of some narrow and bigoted sect, and ask himself : Can I condemn these people who are so obviously full of good intentions ? And if he saw that they darkened the human spirit and prevented it from reaching the stature of manhood which it normally attains, he would judge that sect to be moving at a slower pace than the current of evolution, even though going in the same direction, and therefore not to be beneficial to man or God.

Or again, he might study some unorthodox teaching on morality, and, wanting to discover its trend, view it in the light of biology, and find it to be a deviation from the line by which life has come ; he would then declare that, although it might be progressing at a greater speed and producing changes more rapidly than the slow amelioration of human conscience, yet it was not moving towards the goal of Divine Union, but diverging at a greater or lesser angle from the path of normal advance as determined by prolonging the line by which the race has come. He would then condemn it as out of alignment with evolution.

Or, finally, he might find that different standards prevailed in societies and among men of different states of development. If he were to assess them justly he would have to take into consideration the step of the evolutionary ladder upon which they stood, for principles have to be applied differently at different stages of development, although themselves unchanging. For instance, every primitive man has to be a warrior and a hunter if he is to do his duty to society, but if the predatory impulses persist in civilised society they lead to crime ; it was noticeable how many habitual criminals distinguished themselves in the war, and the remarkable freedom from crime that prevailed while that outlet was available for the adventurous impulses of the race. The professional criminal is by no manner of means invariably a man of ugly temperament or nasty disposition ; he will frequently have heroic virtues. Often he is a man whom civilisation has not suited and who is in rebellion against the cramping conditions of modern life. Had he been the citizen of a frontier colony he might have made good and achieved distinction. He is evil because he is out of date. The impulses which actuate him have ceased to serve a social purpose. He is atavistic, a " throwback " to primitive conditions.

These principles enable us to estimate the Right- and Left-hand Paths and Black and White Occultism. The Right-hand Path is that which prolongs the line of evolution and leads by the most direct route to its goal ; it is the shortest route between the stage at which a man has arrived when he hears the Call, and Divine Union. It will therefore be seen that no one particular route can be laid down as the true Path or system by which every man must come. " The ways to God are as many as the breaths of the sons of men." It is the directness or indirectness of the route that counts.

And again, with regard to Black Occultism, it is impossible to label any operation as at all times and under all circumstances definitely Black or definitely White ; all we can say is, that under certain circumstances it is black or white. Dirt has been defined as misplaced matter, and evil can be defined as misplaced force. Force can be misplaced in time or in space. A thing may be right at one time which is wrong at another. Black Occultism, then, may be defined as misplaced force or out-of-date methods.

The question of out-of-date initiatory methods has been dealt with in an earlier chapter, but we must now take up the question again from the standpoint of the actual training of an aspirant as given in an occult school. Let the aspirant picture himself as standing at the lowest point of an ellipse whose highest point is God ; on his left stretches up the path by which he has descended into matter ; on his right stretches up the path by which he will return to

Spirit. Should he turn and retrace his steps along the path by which he has come, he would be treading the Left-hand Path ; should he press on by the path which evolution will ultimately follow, he would be following the Right-hand Path. By either route he can rise upon the planes, and if he has achieved mastery of a plane by the Right-hand Path, he will be Master of both its aspects, primitive and evolved ; he will, however, have to be careful to keep both its aspects in their right places, but they will not be forbidden to him any longer.

Let us try to make this clear by an example. Supposing without initiation he tried to penetrate into the higher consciousness with the help of drugs ; their action would be to put in abeyance the higher faculties of the mind, thereby enabling the primitive powers of direct psychic perception to function unchecked ; he would indeed penetrate to the astral plane, but would find himself in its limbo, or purgatorial aspect. Should he open the astral senses by the true initiatory methods of the development and extension of consciousness, he would equally obtain access to the astral plane, but into another sphere of it. Should he, however, successfully penetrate that sphere, he would find that when he had achieved mastery over it so that he could move about freely in consciousness thereon, he was able also to penetrate its hells. This power, however, he would never use save for the purpose of " preaching to the spirits in prison." The methods of entering the hells may be used by the Black magician who desires to obtain control over the spirits and employ them for his own evil purposes, and by the White occultist who desires to redeem a soul that may have been drawn into one of the hells;

therefore it cannot be said that these formulæ are definitely evil and should never on any account be used. Black magic concerns itself largely with the evocation of evil spirits, but the White magician may use the same formula to evoke a spirit in order to force it to release its victim. An evocation has to precede an exorcism for the obvious reason that it is impossible to banish a spirit that is not present. That is the reason why many attempts at exorcism prove abortive or merely temporary in their effects ; it is because the operator has not got the nerve for the evocation. No one should expect a man to work out of his degree, or to attempt to use powers which have not been conferred on him, and the wise occultist recognises his limitations and strictly observes them ; but if ritual magic be attempted at all, it ought to be done properly or it is worse than useless. It is not evil in itself, but it can very easily become evil in inexpert hands, because the forces thus evoked readily get out of control.

There is little doubt that evolution has reached the stage when form is beginning to be laid aside. " For as we rise the symbols disappear." The legitimate scope of ritual magic at the present time is limited ; it is rightly used for dealing with certain occult pathologies, especially those which originate in the witchcraft of the past, but it is not a thing to be played with for experimental purposes. Nevertheless, a knowledge of its *modus operandi* and principles is necessary to the neophyte who is opening up the psychic powers, just as a knowledge of swimming is essential to anyone who goes in for boating. The student may be working along lines of spiritual development which do not employ ritual magic, but should an accident occur—and initiation is not fool-proof—he will be precipitated into the sphere where ritual magic operates, and it is the only thing which will extricate him.

The occult powers should be looked upon as a lamp to show the Path to the aspirant, but not as a beacon for him to steer by. They can guide him safely through the unexplored hinterland of the human mind, and without such guidance he is very likely to go astray; but if he turns aside and builds himself a house in the realm of occultism, he will have quitted the Path. His goal is on the heights of Spirit, not in the jungles of mind, but as he must traverse the jungles of mind, he needs equipment for the journey.

CHAPTER XII

THE history of initiation has been touched on very briefly, all too briefly, no doubt, for the general reader unversed in the elements of the subject; it is intended for students, not for propaganda, and the rudiments are taken for granted. It is designed to indicate the way of approach to the Western branch of the great Esoteric Tradition for those who, having made acquaintance with as much of the Secret Wisdom as can be given out publicly, are desirous of continuing their studies in the deeper aspects of the subject.

For this pursuit industry and intellect are not enough; certain conditions of character and certain attitudes of mind are required, and the would-be student must discipline and develop his nature as well as pursue his researches. The Higher Self is the first initiator, none other can put us in touch with the Unseen Masters, and the preliminary work has to be performed subjectively.

It is often asked whether it be possible for initiation to take place without the conscious mind being aware of the experience. To this question the answer is in the negative. Initiation involves the unification of the higher and lower consciousnesses and therefore cannot obviously take place without awareness, or if it could would serve no useful purpose. This, at any rate, is true of the Western Esoteric Tradition wherein the degrees confer actual occult powers which have to be demonstrated to the satisfaction of the magus before the pupil can go on to the higher grades. Whether the same be true of the Eastern Tradition the writer cannot say, not being an initiate of that Tradition, but the evidence points to the same state of affairs prevailing therein, and to the possession of the Siddhis, or occult powers, by all genuine initiates of that Tradition. A different state of affairs, however, arises when a soul incarnated in a Western body seeks, while resident in a Western country and without actual contact with an Eastern Guru, to take an Eastern initiation. In such a case it might be quite possible that awareness of the experience would not succeed in penetrating the physical vehicle. It would then be held, however, that such an experience was only partial, and it would certainly not confer the Siddhis, or Powers of the Degree. Its fruits might be reaped in another incarnation, but hardly in this one. Therefore it is that the initiates of the West have always held that Western methods must be used for Western people, and they have never been denied to suitable applicants, nor yet to any group or society that came with clean hands seeking the contacts. The great Western Esoteric Tradition is a living force; the Western Way is an open road trodden by countless feet, and all who seek it can find it.

The Master is aware of the existence of the pupil, and may even have begun the preliminary training before the pupil is sufficiently psychic to be aware of the presence of the Master. The preliminary training can indeed go on without awareness on

the part of the pupil. The invocation that summoned the Master may have been forgotten; the
quest, though still desired, regarded with despair,
and the seeker believe that he has cried to ears that
were too remote for hearing or even do not exist;
and yet the work may be going steadily forward
upon his higher self, beyond the range of brain
consciousness. Let him not despair, but keep on
with his aspiration, and in due course he shall reap if
he fail not. Day by day the higher consciousness
is being pushed nearer and nearer to the threshold;
the great forces that the Masters let loose upon the
soul that opens itself to Them is filling its depths
like a spring flowing into a reservoir; slowly the
waters gather head behind the barrier that separates
subconsciousness from consciousness, and when
the time is ripe the initiator lays his hand upon the
lever that operates the sluices and the water flows in
its appointed channel.

The operation, therefore, is a twofold one, and is
performed upon two planes simultaneously, just as a
tunnel through a mountain is bored from both ends
at once. And just as in the driving of a tunnel, it
depends upon the skill of the engineers and the
accuracy of their instruments whether the two
cuttings shall meet or miss each other in the depths
of the mountain, so it depends upon the psycholo-
gical skill of the teacher as to whether the two lines
of development shall meet or miss each other in the
depths of the aspirant's subconsciousness. His
duty it is to see that the training of the personality
and conscious mind shall be conducted in such a
way that the crooked places shall be made straight
and the Path of the Soul be brought into alignment
with the Path of the Power of the Spirit descending

like a lightning-flash. If this be not done, the junction between the two Paths may have to be effected by means of just such an S-bend as disfigured one of the earlier Alpine tunnels. Such a twisting of the path of power is always a source of danger, for it is the tendency of any force to go straight on, and it may fail to take the bend. Such a force, ploughing a track through consciousness and oversetting all that lies in its course, is known to occultists as a tort, and is the cause of many pathologies of both mind, morals and body. The risk of such an occurrence is greatly lessened when the Path is trodden under the guidance of a reliable teacher. He will know the angle of incidence of the initiatory force and can instruct his pupil how to bring his state of consciousness into alignment with it.

How shall he who has glimpsed the possibility of the Great Work find a Master who shall train him for its performance ? This is the supreme question for the earnest seeker. But remember this : treading the Path is very different from studying the map. The map may be studied by lamplight at the fireside, the Path is trodden out in the wind and darkness of the barren places of the soul; for the Path is within, and leads from brain consciousness, through subconsciousness, to superconsciousness. It is, nevertheless, by no manner of means subjective, and it is concerning the objective aspect of the quest that the student will no doubt be curious.

Let us consider the spiritual history of one who sets out on the quest, and note the stages through which he will pass.

First there comes the formulation of the concept ; he conceives the idea of initiation and the ideal of the Master's service and desires to make his dedication.

But is desire enough? Yes, it is enough *if it is strong enough and long enough*; if it continues unwavering and unshaken through all the testing of the soul that shall try its fibre, through the purgation that shall purify it for the Master's contacting, and through the toil of the training that shall fit it for the Master's service; if the desire for initiation continue unwavering through all this, it shall bring the pupil to the feet of the Master.

But how few achieve or even realise the strength of the desire that is needed to bring about initiation. The beautiful Eastern tradition tells of the Master who held his chela under water till he was half-drowned, and told him that when he desired light as fervently as he desired air he would receive it; and the Western story tells of the man who sold all he had in order to buy the pearl of great price. He who sets foot upon the Path may take nothing with him; naked are we born into the world, and naked we pass out of it into the higher consciousness. The " heavenly homesick " are many, but those who will endure the divine journey are few. It is impossible to make the best of both worlds, for where our treasure is there will our heart be also.

It is only those for whom the lust of the flesh and the desire of the eyes and the pride of life have ceased to have any significance who will essay the Path that leads to the heights, and for them the journey will not be hard, because they travel light. He who goes empty-handed treads easily; it is the great burden of egoistical necessities that renders the way toilsome.

Presently there comes to the soul a bitter period of conflict. It has glimpsed the divine ideal, it has drunk of the living waters of the spirit, and these have begotten in it a thirst which cannot be slaked upon earth ; having known reality, it cannot find rest in appearances ; and yet it has not exhausted the delights of matter. It is best that such an one should seriously count the cost before embarking upon the Great Quest and calling upon the Masters for aid in his search. For the Masters will take him at his word if he invokes them, and cause him to pass through the flame of circumstance so that all dross may be purged from his character ; but if the ore of his nature be poor in spiritual metal, the conflagration thus caused will generate such heat that the gold will fuse and run, and the form of that man be lost. It is the desireless man alone who passes into the Great Freedom, and when one who is ruled by desires essays the passage, these desires, being torn up by the roots, cause the soul to bleed. It is better that a ripening of the spirit should be achieved so that it parts with its fleshly desires naturally by outgrowing them, rather than do violence to the instincts of nature. It is not the suppression but the outgrowing of desires that we should seek ; ripe fruit parts readily from the stem, and the man who has learned the lessons that life teaches will pass on without repining. An incomplete, abortive experience of life is not a good foundation for illumination.

Initiation cannot be obtained in less than three incarnations of steadily directed effort. In the first incarnation the soul conceives the ideal and nurses it in secret, fulfilling all the duties of humanity in humility and patience, thus building character ; in the second incarnation the soul undergoes testing and purgation and has to meet its karma—this is sometimes spoken of as the seed incarnation ; and in the third incarnation it rapidly recapitulates the development attained in the other two and is ready for the Path.

Each individual who conceives the ideal of initiation has to ascertain whether consciousness is being awakened for the first time, or whether memory is returning from the depths of the sub-consciousness after the inter-natal sleep ; it is here that the advice of a teacher who can read the Records is very necessary, for an imagination fired by the lust of adventure or the spirit of emulation may lead the aspirant grievously astray, causing him to venture in out of his depth. It may also happen that the previous preparatory life may not have fulfilled its purpose and the preparation thus be incomplete ; the work has then to be done over again before further advance can be made. Finally, there are many souls who have been initiated in the past but have been led aside into Black Magic or failed in a test, and must then laboriously climb back up the ground that has been lost ; such souls are often psychic but have no knowledge of occultism ; the subtle senses that have been developed may remain, but the contacts are broken and the memories obliterated by the Master who has been betrayed ; for these the Path is forbidden until expiation has been completed and the wrong redressed ; their own instinct is the best guide in this matter, for they will know with an unerring certainty when the invisible barrier is down and they are free to go forward.

The aspiration of the soul for initiation should be formulated and held with an unswerving determination ; it should be meditated upon and brooded over in the night watches, and every action of the waking hours dedicated to the perfecting of character and the service of humanity, and, through it, of the Masters; but the soul should wait in humility for psychic experiences, not seeking to project itself out into the astral spaces where it has neither guide, chart nor compass. In due season, when the time is ripe, it shall indeed travel the astral ways, but under the care of a guide, and not alone.

The Masters receive souls as pupils, not for the benefit of the soul, but for the benefit of the Great Work; a man is not trained for the sake of his curiosity or enthusiasm, but only in so far as he is of value as a servant; it is for this reason that a selfless desire to serve is the surest path to the Master; no one who desires knowledge or power for its own sake ever succeeds in obtaining the innermost essence of it. He may become a magician, or an astral seer, or even possess deep intuitional wisdom, but the spiritual Light of the Innermost is unlit. Let us make no mistake, it is the Spirit which is the goal of the quest; all else is a means to an end, all else an appearance, not a reality; and though appearances may not necessarily be delusive, but rather a true and accurate symbolism and system of correspondences, they cannot satisfy the hunger of the spiritual nature after the Spirit of God. The astral body functions on the astral plane, and the mental body wakes to consciousness on the mental plane when it receives its initiation, but the spiritual body must needs wake to the world of Spirit before the sevenfold man is completed. Neither mentality nor emotion will satisfy the needs of the spirit.

In Union with the Divine, which the Western esotericist conceives of as being the supreme initiation, the Spark of Divine Spirit, which is to man what the grain of sand is to the pearl, wakes into consciousness within the fully-formed sixth-plane body of concrete spirit; this is the first of the cosmic initiations, because the Divine Spark, being, meta-phorically speaking, of the Plane of God, has passed beyond the Ring Pass-not of the projected universe into the noumenal Cosmos where the consciousness of the Great Entity dwells.

This supreme spiritual ideal must never be lost sight of in all the long course of the Path : it alone is the goal, for nothing else can give the final and full completion. If this landmark be kept always before the eyes, the traveller will not wander from the way, for although his journey must be by stages and through differing kinds of country, and although the discipline of each stage must be undergone in order to build up the completion of the soul, he must never pause or rest until he has reached the ultimate Divine Union; neither must he, at any stage of the Path, turn aside and build a house, thinking that in the perfection of that phase he shall find completion. Each ridge he climbs will but reveal the ridge be-yond, and from each crest he must descend into the valley of humiliation in order to mount the ridge of the next discipline. Neither astral sight nor magical powers are ends in themselves, but rather subserve the ends of the Adept, who, unless he has also the powers of the spirit, is but as sounding brass and a tinkling cymbal; but yet, if he have the things of the spirit and have not these also, he must needs be of those who wait in subjective bliss for the end of the Day of Manifestation, for without the Powers of the Planes he cannot return to help humanity on its upward path; he must be a magician if he is going to be a Master, for without the occult arts he cannot pass from plane to plane. This is a very important point and one to be seriously considered in the choice of an esoteric school or teacher.

Let us now consider the actual stages in the training of the seeker who, having formulated a true ideal, has caused his light to shine forth in the dark places of the world. By thinking of the Masters we attract their attention, and it is unbelievably easy to establish a magnetic link with those who are always more ready to give than we are to receive ; and if any one, after thinking about the Masters and formulating a wish to be accepted as a pupil, finds that the circumstances of his life are beginning to blow up for storm, he will know that his application has been accepted and that the preliminary tests have begun. At every point in his life he will be tested for freedom from desire. Now it must not be thought that the service of the Masters necessarily means bankruptcy and bereavement ; a man may have vast wealth and yet the things that money can buy may mean so little to him that he never troubles to buy them, leading a life of great simplicity and using the whole of his vast resources in selfless service, asking neither reward nor thanks. Such an one would feel relief rather than loss were he deprived of his fortune. But if there is one who, even with the narrowest means, clings desperately to his slender security, he will be tested by financial loss until he realises that, if we take the Master at His word and seek first the Kingdom of Heaven and its righteousness, all these things are added unto us.

The Master Jesus is the Master of Compassion, and His Kingdom is the Kingdom of Love, but if we love any creature or thing with a purely personal love, a love that enjoys the sensation of loving rather han the good of the beloved, we shall surely be tested by the withdrawal of the thing desired. But if we love with a love so completely selfless that we would stand aside without a pang if the beloved one might thereby receive a greater good than it is in our power to bestow, then we love with the Greater Love which shall not be taken away, neither can height nor depth nor any other creature sunder us from the object of our love.

Do not let it be thought that in the sacrifices of the Path any duty has to be put aside ; it is not duties, but desires that have to be foregone. Every legitimate duty has to be fulfilled, not evaded, and every human debt paid before we are free to enter upon the dedication which the study of the Secret Wisdom involves. There are, however, many ways to the Masters of Wisdom, and one of them is the Path of the Hearth-fire, whereby through the fulfilling of household duties in love, initiation is won. The sacred duties of the home are the steps on the Path, and it often falls to the lot of those who in past incarnations have pursued knowledge for its own sake rather than for service that they should follow this discipline. Let these dedicate themselves to it as to the Master, but using all leisure to study faithfully and provide the necessary basis of knowledge, and let their motto be :

> " Earn the means first, God surely will contrive
> Use for our earning."

Wherever the soul finds itself, from that point must it start upon its journey ; no one can stand in the shoes of another. The soul must always " make good " on that which lies to its hand before it enters upon the Path. If that soul finds itself as a clerk or a cook, it must become an efficient clerk or a good cook ; the Masters have as little use for incompetence as they have for sin, and if we are incompetent in the discharge of any section of our undertakings, a substratum of weakness will underlie the whole nature, and the tests of the Path will find it out.

In due course the time will come when the seeker, having safely undergone the preliminary tests, finds the Path proper opening up before him ; having made the utmost of the means at his disposal and exhausted them, further opportunities are given him. The exhaustion of material placed to hand for his practice is a very important point in connection with advancement. A seeker may sigh for books beyond his means, and feel unable to advance in his studies for lack of them, but has he exhausted the possibilities of the municipal free library ? Or he may desire deep teaching on meditation, but has he learnt to keep his head during the rush hours of his business ? All these things are used by the Masters as discipline, and They observe the proficiency of the pupil in these things before They advance him, and one of the surest tests is the tidiness of the room a person occupies and the orderly conduct of his affairs ; an occultist needs an even temper and an iron nerve, and there are few walks in life that cannot be made to afford opportunities for the development of essential preliminaries.

All having been done, then, that the seeker can do in solitude, the Star Lodge under which his Path is being taken allots to him a Guide. The office of Guide is one of the first that is filled by a soul that has advanced beyond incarnation in matter. After the last death of the body of one who has dedicated himself to the service of the Masters, the newly-liberated soul is employed in the great humanitarian work that goes on on the astral plane ; this work is well known to all engaged in spiritualistic research, and need not be entered into in detail in these pages, and the office of Guide is one of its sub-divisions.

A guide acts as messenger between the Master and the pupil, conveying instruction by means of telepathic suggestion to the consciousness of the soul in his care ; he also has the task of protecting his charge during his first expeditions on to the inner planes, safeguarding him during the difficult moments of transition from one plane to another and supporting him until he has learnt skill in making the transition through the states of consciousness.

For a period varying from a few months to several years the relation of Guide and seeker continues, and by the end of it they are as well acquainted with each other as any other pair of friends. Guides are simply human beings of a lofty type who have not got physical bodies, and the personality is that of the last incarnation. A time may come, however, when the Guide is ready to advance to higher work but the seeker is not yet ready for the next stage ; a new Guide will then be allotted to him and the other will withdraw, though he may from time to time visit his erstwhile charge, for these friendships of the inner planes are just as real as those of the earth-plane.

When the time comes, however, that the pupil is able to come and go between the planes with confidence and sureness and can himself receive the commands of his Master, he no longer needs the help of his Guide, who is then withdrawn for other work.

Many souls are trained entirely from the inner planes in this way, but there are others which do not so readily develop psychism, and for them another method is used. The Guide will act as go-between from the pupil who is to be trained to another servant of the same Master who has already been trained in the physical body, and will place the student under a teacher. Now a teacher is not a master, and no one worthy of the name would claim the title : his function is to inform the pupil, not to dominate him.

A teacher, adequately to fulfil his function, must be a psychic, and it is worse than useless for the aspirant to study with any occultist who is not, for how shall the blind lead the blind ? Psychism is the eyes of the soul on the planes of form, and there must be adequate astral vision if the student is to be properly handled and well protected.

An occult student is in as much need of protection during the early stages of his training as a hermit crab that has left one shell to search for another, otherwise he will develop nerve trouble and exhaustion ; these complaints are not a *sine quâ non* of occult development, neither do they show the spirituality of the nature, but are a sign of faulty training ; they do not redound to the credit of the student but to the discredit of the teacher. No occult work should be attempted by a person in a devitalised or unbalanced condition ; everything must be put aside until he has recovered his physical fitness, and it is the duty of the teacher to look after the physical condition of the pupil as carefully as after his spiritual condition.

The teacher knows the pupil by the seal of the Master which is stamped on the aura just above the head, but how is the pupil to know the teacher and

be sure that he is not in the hands of a charlatan ?
Firstly because the teacher will ask him for no
money for his instruction.   This is the supreme test
of an occult teacher and effectually rules out the
mercenary.   A man, however, may be well-inten-
tioned and idealistic, but nevertheless a fool ; how
is the pupil to know that he is not getting into the
hands of an incompetent ?   He must exercise the
same care and discretion as he would in transacting
any important business matter on the physical plane ;
he must make enquiries as to the reputation and
record of the person into whose hands he proposes
to commit his spiritual life.   He must observe closely
the character, outlook and type of the members of
the group by whom the teacher is surrounded, for
here will be seen the clearest indication of the nature
of the teaching given, and it is an indication that
cannot lie.   " By their fruits ye shall know them."
And the wayfaring man, though a fool, knows the
fruits of the Spirit when he sees them.   Purity and
peace, a sane mind in a sound body ;   charity of
thought and action as well as of speech and printing ;
order and cleanliness of both mind and environment ;
fair dealing and the honourable meeting of obligations ;   and, above all, the simple kindliness that
sweetens human intercourse, " against these there
is no law," but where these are lacking, beware.

Occult training should build nobility of character
and balance of mind.   If it fails to do this there is
something amiss.   What shall it profit a man if he
sees the heavens open and lose his reason ?   It is
better to have five senses and sanity than psychism
and a lack of balance.   A teacher of any system of
occult training can only be justified by results.
Good intentions may serve to protect the individual

who ventures into the Unseen in search of knowledge for himself, but they are not sufficient equipment for the one who undertakes to train another.

Some cry " Peace, peace," where there is no peace, refusing to see signs of mental and physical deterioration in their pupils, and regarding the symptoms of nervous tension as incipient psychism. Unskilled in the processes of the mind, they fail to recognise dissociation and hallucination when they see them, regarding abnormal phenomena as evidence of unfolding powers. Seership is an integration of the individuality, not a disintegration of the personality. The great problem that always besets the seer is the problem of synthesis, the maintenance of open communications between the higher and lower self, and the translation of the abstract into the concrete so that it may be assimilable by consciousness ; and no system of training which tends to loosen the cohesion of the personality can produce satisfactory results.

Other teachers, accustomed to operate an ineffectual system, suddenly lose their heads when an exceptionally sensitive pupil begins to get results and naturally turns to them for explanation and guidance. Not being psychic themselves, they are unable to see what the pupil sees, and if all does not go smoothly (and under such circumstances it is not very likely to go smoothly), they become panic-stricken and drop the pupil like a hot coal. The condition of such an one is deplorable, and generally ends in severe breakdown or even insanity. The condition of such a teacher is not less deplorable, though the karmic results may not manifest so quickly. It cannot be repeated too often that an iron nerve is needed for all occult operations, and especially for an initiation, and unless an occultist has the faculty to read the records and discern the karma of an applicant and to read the aura and discern the condition, he should not undertake to train a pupil in esoteric science.

Every true initiator knows that he has to share in the karma that shall be generated by any pupil he trains ; if that pupil makes good use of his knowledge and does well, the initiator is thereby advanced ; a highly evolved group is of incalculable value to any occultist, hence the folly of withholding advancement out of jealousy. On the other hand, the abuse of occult power has a disastrous effect not only on the person who does it, but on the group in which he was trained. Just as the pupil should be careful in placing himself in the hands of a teacher, so the teacher has just as great need to be careful in the acceptance of a pupil, and the applicant must be prepared to submit to tests before he is trusted. He should be wary of the ever-open door ; those who have treasures, guard them.

He must remember, however, that the teacher cannot reveal his system to the unobligated, and the more he knows the less he will be inclined to tell, and even the most cautious must be prepared to take something on trust ; but if, considering the teacher, he feels that he desires to become even as he, then he will be safe in enrolling himself. But if, after considering the teacher, he feels that he must reject the character while absorbing the knowledge, he will be very unwise to have any dealings at all with that person, because he will find *that in actual practice he is unable to maintain the distinction.*

A man may teach natural science without any considerations of personal character entering into the matter, but not so with occult science. The essence of occult training does not lie in what is taught, but in the influences that emanate from the teacher and gradually tune the pupil to higher and higher vibrations. The teacher has to transmit the forces of the Master until the pupil becomes *en rapport* with that Master : it is in this that the real value of the training lies, not in the information that is communicated ; everybody teaches much the same things, some a little more, some a little less ; there is no great divergence between the different schools, but there is an immense difference in their respective vitality and purity.

If a teacher has evil or unsublimated aspects in his own nature, these aspects will put him in touch with the corresponding potencies in the unseen world, and when he seeks to bring through the force of his Master, he will be working on a mixed contact, and the results for the pupil will be good and evil inextricably blended. Under such circumstances the teacher tends more and more to be dissociated from his Master, and is therefore working upon a falling tide, and as the higher forces fail, the lower come more into evidence. Such an one is an exceedingly dangerous acquaintance for anyone who is at all sensitive.

However strong he may feel himself to be, no pupil may hope to be stronger than his teacher, for if the latter does not know more than he, why go to him ? Never believe that you will be able to sort out the wheat from the tares before the harvest. If the teacher is a man of impure life you cannot fail to be involved in impurity ; if he be unscrupulous, you will be sacrificed to his love of power or gain.

I have heard it argued that the willingness to face the odium of association with evil-doers is one of the tests of the Path. To stand by the teacher through good and ill *report* is indeed a test, but to condone evil action is not; the test in such a case is of a contrary nature. Are you prepared to lose your chance of initiation rather than receive it from unclean hands? Are you prepared to refuse the Waters of Life if they are polluted with dirt? On the answer to these questions much depends. Is it the test that you should swallow the dirt for the sake of the teaching? Or is it that you should reject the opportunity on account of the dirt? Follow your instinct. It will lead you to the place where you belong.

But remember this: no one has the power to give you initiation or deny it to you; as soon as you are entitled to it you claim it by right, not by grace. If one channel closes, another will open up. Claim your initiation from the Masters, not from any Lodge, Fraternity, or Order upon the physical plane; and although the vote of such an assembly has the power to close any particular Lodge to you, it has not the power to close the Order if that Order be a true occult fraternity, for in such case the decision does not rest with those upon this plane, but with Those upon the Inner Planes whence the Order derives its power. If those who are the guardians of the gates on the physical side persistently deny access to those to whom it is due, the stream of force issuing through those gates will be deflected to another channel, a bare and boulder-strewn bed will lie where there once had been a navigable course, and the Waters of Life will flow elsewhere; but the Waters of Life will not cease to flow because human judgment declares them private.   No seeker after truth need fear human judgment ; the issue lies between him and his Master and none other. If he fit himself for initiation he will receive it, if not from one hand, then from another, and if he were not ready for it the greatest Adept in the cosmos would be unable to bestow it on him.

Never hesitate to take your stand boldly upon a principle in occult matters, for you are dealing in principles, and if you take not your stand upon these, where shall you set your foot and find it firm ? Expediency is a most dangerous double-edged weapon ; never risk it.   In all moments of difficulty and danger, rise on to a higher plane, and in spiritual principles find the solution of astral difficulties.   Never be guided by anybody's opinion in seeking the solution of an occult problem.   Look within, and seek to hear the still small voice of conscience, for it shall be to you the Voice of the Master. But before so listening, invoke the Master, and ring yourself about with the sacred circle of His power, drawing it in the air with your finger while invoking the Name ; *for there is such a thing as telepathic suggestion*, and if you have reason to believe that this is at work, if you find ideas obtruding themselves in your mind which would not normally find tolerance there, then you would do well to conduct the meditation that shall make clear your path in a church where the Blessed Sacrament is reserved, for into that Presence and potency can come nothing that maketh a lie.

CHAPTER XIII

For those of highly developed will and consciousness it is possible to obtain access to the source of the Secret Wisdom by purely intuitional and meditative methods, but a considerable degree of advancement in these methods is necessary before this is possible. There are many, however, who have a sincere desire for such knowledge, and who have already achieved the development of character which entitles them to receive it, but who cannot obtain it owing to a lack of the necessary technique of consciousness which renders it accessible to purely meditative methods. For these there exists a school of training which, although it does not claim to open the gate of the unseen worlds, can show where that gate is and give the key that will unlock it when the pupil has trodden the path that brings him to it. More than this no one can do, unless he chooses to make use of drugs and hypnosis and pay the price that these exact.

As has already been said: " The ways to God are as many as the breaths of the sons of men." There are seven known Paths, though not all are in function as Ways of Initiation at the present time, and upon each Path are many schools. The choice of a school depends upon temperament, for all those that are not of the Left-hand Path teach an aspect or degree of the eternal Truth which is universally valid. A school of esotericism usually arises in connection with some special realisation of the Truth, which it sometimes stresses beyond its due proportion to life as a whole, but there will never be found any teaching which has the power to hold together a body of earnest seekers which has not a spark of the divine fire at its heart; therefore respect should be given to all who seek in sincerity, however far from the goal they may appear to be, and all who are engaged in the great Quest should rather try to see the vision which a brother has glimpsed than the special errors to which he has fallen a victim.

No enunciation of the Truth will ever be complete, no method of training will ever be suitable to all temperaments, no one can do more than mark out the little plot of Infinity which he intends to cultivate, and thrust in the spade, trusting that the soil may eventually be fruitful and free from weeds so far as the bounds he has set himself extend; but although labour is essential to any enterprise, it is God who giveth the increase. A fraternity which has no illumination save the inspiration of its founder is limited by the capacity of his personality, and will be a burnt-out cinder when the personality is withdrawn. An esoteric school differs from all other schools in the fact that though, like them, its wisdom may be stored in its library, its power lies in its contacts with the Inner Worlds, and unless it has these contacts it cannot give its pupils the power to put theory into practice. All schools of the Right-hand Path teach the same principles, but they differ very much in their power to apply them. Some maintain that it should be enough for us to know the theory, and that to attempt its practical application is a dangerous presumption; others maintain that all experience is purely subjective. This, of course, may be true for the pupils of these schools, but there is no need for those foxes which have tails to cut them off.

Unless the study of esoteric science yields fruits of practical application it is unworthy of the pursuit of any serious-minded person, and unless these fruits be the fruits of the spirit it is unworthy the study of any spiritually-minded person. Man has four aspects—physical, emotional, intellectual and spiritual—and any method of training should take account of all four if it is to produce that balance of nature which alone can give stability. Psychism is often unfortunately associated with instability, but nothing but stability and fortitude are compatible with the exercise of the occult powers.

Occultism is not fool-proof; it makes heavy demands upon the spiritual stamina of those who elect to study it, but if pursued under the right conditions it can be productive of good without any inevitable alloy of evil. It is no pursuit for either the weak or the timorous, however pure their intentions may be, neither is it a wholesome interest for the immature; as maturity is a matter of individual development, it is difficult to draw a hard and fast line, but the writer never cares to see anyone under the age of twenty-five taking an interest in these subjects. The first quarter-century of life should be given to the physical plane; if attention is turned to the inner planes prematurely, it tends to withdraw energy from the outer planes before the full development of brain-consciousness has been attained, and that person will have insufficient power

of extroversion, and a tendency to become per-
manently introvert, whereas the properly trained
occultist should maintain a balanced rhythm between the two aspects of consciousness.

Balance is the keynote of all true esoteric training ; to the ill-balanced nature the higher wisdom
is nothing but a danger ; stability is as necessary as
purity upon the Path. A sensitive is a very different
kind of person from an occultist ; and the type of
training which will develop a sensitive is very
different from that which is employed to train an
occultist. Those who adventure into the unseen
worlds may be divided into three classes, sensitives
and mediums, mystics, and occultists. Sensitives
and mediums are classed together, because the latter
is but a fuller development of the former ; both are
of the negative or purely receptive aspect of the
higher consciousness ; both are passive, affected by
that which is external to the self, without power to
control it ; whereas both occultist and mystic
are intensely active. The powers of both sensitive
and medium should form part of the armoury of a
fully-trained occultist ; he should be able to perceive
the unseen as clearly as can a sensitive, and he should
be able upon occasion to act as transmitter of communications from one plane to another, but he also
needs to be so very much more. His ego should be
like the conductor of an orchestra in which the
faculties of psychism and mediumship are among
the instruments at his command, which he can call
upon or silence at will. It is the fashion among
occultists to decry the phenomena of the séance
room, phenomena with which they have often no
first-hand acquaintance, and in this, in my opinion,
they do the spiritualist an injustice. Spiritualism

is simply empirical occultism; and though the occultist would shrink from the risks the spiritualist sometimes takes without being aware of what he is doing, and though the latter frequently owes his safety to the fact that he is paddling in shallow water, there is no occasion for mutual recrimination. Each has much to give the other. The experiments of the séance room are forbidden to the lesser degrees of occultism, not because they are wicked, but because they are risky for an occultist owing to the potencies with which he is in touch; the possessor of an electric torch can experiment with its mechanism in a way that would be unwise for a person whose lamp was connected up with a power station.

It is amusing to note that, while the occultist decries the spiritualist, the mystic looks askance at the occultist; yet a mystic is simply an introvert occultist, and the occultist an extrovert mystic. Both aim at the same goal, though they seek it by different methods. The difference between them is of temperament, not of ideal. When the scientific temperament approaches the Unseen, it chooses the Occult Path of development, and when the artistic temperament approaches the Unseen, it chooses the Mystic Path; one progresses through right knowing, and the other through right feeling, and both meet in the end. Difference of method should never blind us to unity of aim.

The mystic pursues a solitary path, even when he is a member of a community; his visions are for himself alone, and he has often but little power to teach that which he has himself learnt. He reaches the heights of the spirit and dwells there apart; his experience is a personal one, and cannot be communicated to others. He is essentially the artistic temperament working upon the things of the spirit ; creative, joyous, and inspiring to those who can appreciate his art because they are akin to him in nature. Esotericism, without a touch of mystic rapture, would be as drab as a culture that had no place for the beautiful; but a spiritual culture which is purely mystical has little relation to the problems of humanity and no message for the common man.

Occultism, on the other hand, is of the intellect. The occult path is followed in co-operation with others, because its heights are achieved by means of group-work and the use of ritual.

We might well speak of the mystic art and the occult science ; and in so speaking we are reminded that every art is based upon a science, and every applied science partakes of the nature of an art. The highest development is attained when the mystic has the knowledge and technique of an occultist, or when the occultist is at heart a mystic. The mystic can then express the teachings of the spirit in terms of the intellect and so render them available for those who have no higher consciousness than that of the mind ; and the occultist who shares in the things of the spirit will have that element of devotion in his nature which is so often lacking in those in whom the intellect is dominant. Without this element the final synthesis is impossible ; he will only be as the exoteric philosopher who follows an ever-receding horizon, because he only studies phenomena by means of the effect they produce upon the senses. Noumenal consciousness, which is the ultimate aim of the esotericist, is only possible to those who can actually unite with that which they wish to know. The ultimate object of realisation is the Logos by whose fiat all things are ; union with the Divine can only take place through devotion, and union with the Divine is the ultimate synthesis. To this all paths lead, and in this all aims find their realisation. The mystic seeks a state of feeling in which he shall be at one with God, and the occultist seeks a state of knowing in which he shall have a complete realisation of truth ; both of these can know God, but neither can know God in His entirety.

Therefore it is that in the Lesser Mysteries the neophyte whose temperament leans towards occultism is made to follow the Mystic Way, and the mystic is forced on to the Occult Path ; it is not until the Greater Mysteries are reached that either is permitted to follow his natural bent. This is done to ensure balanced development.

CHAPTER XIV

" IF the light in thee be darkness, how great is that darkness." It is the Christ within who is the First Initiator. The entrance to the Path is to be sought within, not without, for it is a state of exalted consciousness. But once that consciousness is attained, the Path is objective as well as subjective. Some teachers declare the Path to be entirely subjective, saying that the aim of initiation is the perfecting of man ; others teach that initiation is an astral experience ; while popular thought often believes that the man who seeks initiation will find it in some remote district behind high walls. None of these concepts contains the whole truth, but there is an element of truth in all of them.

In order to attain to initiation the raising of consciousness to a degree higher than is common among the average of humanity is necessary. Consciousness must not only transcend the five physical senses, but it must also transcend ordinary psychism if the experience which is connoted by the term initiation in these pages is to be achieved. Initiation is a spiritual, not an astral experience; the candidate shifts the focus of his consciousness from the personality, the unit of incarnation, to the individuality, the immortal ego, or unit of evolution, and the consciousness of the individuality, being abstract, is able to apprehend the things of the spirit which have no manifestation on the planes of form.

The initiate transfers the focus of his consciousness from the personality to the individuality, and therefore things which are hidden from the ordinary man are perceptible to him. He lives in an evolution, not in an incarnation, and consequently all his values are changed. He can see deeply into the realm of causes, perceiving events brewing on the inner planes long before they become manifest on the outer; therefore he has the gift of prophecy. Seeing causes, he can often control them; therefore he appears to have magical powers. Operating upon the higher planes, which act as controlling-levels to the lower planes, he can balance force against force by throwing his will into the scale, and so change the issue of events on the physical plane. These things it is which cause the initiate to be regarded as possessed of magical powers; but these powers are not of the nature of magic; the initiate achieves his ends by employing the powers of his higher self on the higher planes, even as does the wayfaring man whose prayer achieves an answer.

The Path which leads to initiation is the way of life which enables a man to rise above the desires and limitations of his personality and live in his higher self, and the experience of initiation is the transference of consciousness from the personality to the individuality.

A man sets foot upon the Path immediately he desires to do so. This is the first step, and a very simple one. But it is only by continuation of desire that he sets one foot before another, which is the treading of the Path. It is very few souls who maintain a sufficiently steadfast desire to enable them to

make perceptible progress; but desire, steadily
continued, will presently be found to have achieved
the desired aim, and the candidate will be placed
in possession of the necessary knowledge to enable
him to make purposive progress and to direct his
efforts to a definite end. It is for this reason that
the Masters found and support such organisations
as the Theosophical Society, the Anthroposophical
Society, the Rosicrucian Fellowship, and many
others, less well known but not less useful, and to all
such, those who have seen the dawn should give
their support out of gratitude for the light they
have themselves received and in order that the Path
may be made easier for others.

Through the books and lectures of such societies
as these the candidate will learn that his dream has
a foundation in fact, and that his inner urge is
founded on a true instinct; they will give him a
map of the Path, though no one but himself can
tread it. From them he will learn of the origin of
man as a divine potentiality, of his evolution
through the sevenfold experiences of form, and of
his ultimate transcendence of form in the development of the divine actuality; he will learn of the
seven planes and the possibilities of those planes,
and he will also learn of the existence of the Masters.

Having learnt of all these things, having, as it
were, acquired the theory of esoteric science, how is
the candidate to translate that theory into practice ?
How is he personally to experience that of which he
reads ? He can achieve the perception of the astral
plane by the use of auto-hypnosis and drugs; the
method is simple, but the consequences are disastrous
to the higher self. He can also bring the astral into
manifestation on the physical plane by the use of

magic. The knowledge of these methods, however, is carefully guarded and not easily obtained, neither may it safely be used by anyone except an Adept.

The way to attain personal knowledge of the higher worlds may easily be told, though it may not so easily be practised. The senses of the individuality can cognise these worlds ; if therefore the higher aspects of man, the spiritual nature and the power of abstract thought, be cultivated until they have attained a considerable degree of development, and if the focus of consciousness be then shifted from the personality, the unit of incarnation, to the individuality, the unit of evolution, it will be found possible to further develop these aspects of the nature until the universe shall be apprehended in terms of abstract thought and spiritual intuition. The shift of the focus of consciousness is attained by shifting the focus of desire from the things of the senses to the things of the spirit. It is not enough that the will should be directed to a spiritual objective ; a stage of development must be reached at which the spontaneous desires are also directed there. Many would-be initiates make the mistake of thinking that the will to initiation is sufficient, but this is not the case ; the majority of the desires of the nature, both conscious and subconscious, must be turned away from the things of sense towards the things of the spirit ; and as the subconscious mind contains much that concerns the childhood of the race and tends towards matter in its densest forms, it is necessary to extend consciousness far into what is usually the territory of the subconsciousness in order to secure the assimilation of the instinctive desires to the aims of the spiritual nature.

In order to achieve this assimilation we must

first know ourselves in our most primitive aspects, and then sublimate those aspects till they can be assimilated to the personality ; for not until the personality has itself been integrated can it deliberately, of its own enlightened volition, seek the fulfilment of its life in the ideals of the individuality. This is the apotheosis of the personality ; it is for this that the hunger of the soul is for ever crying out, for it can find no satisfaction in the things of sense. Union with the divine aspect of the self, the God within, must precede awareness of the God of the Whole of which it is but a part. The spiritual level of man's nature is but a circumscribed portion of the One Spirit, the All, the Noumenal aspect of manifestation. For that which is itself Noumenal, or an underlying actuality, there can be no satisfaction in that which is phenomenal, or of the nature of projected experience. The spark of the Divine Light, which is the nucleus of the reincarnating ego, or individuality, must associate with its equals if it is to know companionship ; the spiritual aspect of the herd instinct can only achieve satisfaction through union with Spirit ; it has no abiding place in the world of phenomena, and if consciousness has ever been raised to the apprehension of spiritual realities apart from experiences in the world of form, it will never again accept anything as valid which has not a nucleus of such noumenal actuality. Such a reality, once experienced, bringing, as it does, the complete satisfaction of life itself, not of any satiated appetite, forms the type of all future satisfaction and determines its validity. Should such an experience ever have taken place in the history of the incarnating ego, it will never be forgotten, but will be carried foward life after life and imprinted upon the subconsciousness of the personality, the unit of incarnation, until such time as evolution shall render it possible for that which is ultra-conscious to be made conscious.

The first initiation consists of the flash of cosmic consciousness wherein the ego sees with the eyes of the spirit instead of the eyes of the flesh. This is only achieved by exaltation of consciousness, and comes from within. But such an experience having been known, to reproduce it in any subsequent incarnation it is only necessary to link consciousness with subconsciousness by means of an association-chain in order to bring this particular aspect of subconscious content into conscious awareness. This is achieved by means of ritual initiation, and the symbolism of the ritual employed is designed to carry consciousness along the appropriate association-chain which shall end in the memory of the Light of Reality.

Ritual initiation can do no more than this, but it is sufficient; for in the Great Light, Masterhood is comprised. The developed psychic or fully trained magician may become an Adept upon all the planes of the cube of manifestation, but beyond lies something more, which has its affinities with that which, in relation to the solar universe, is unmanifest, being Cosmic. No one can be called an initiate who has not experienced cosmic consciousness. To pass through the degrees of the Greater Mysteries without it may mean no more than a psychic upheaval, the eyes being blinded by excess of light which consciousness possesses no symbol to interpret; on the other hand, the neophyte, if properly prepared, may see the Light behind the symbols and receive illumination.

If the preceding pages are to be understood, they must not be interpreted in their literal or verbal meaning. Those things which they are intended to describe have no words or images in the language to represent them. In order to arrive at their meaning the reader must interpret them by means of analogous experiences of his own. If he has no analogous experience, he will not receive the impression it is intended to convey, and will not unreasonably account these things foolishness. To such an one I can offer nothing; evolutionary time must do its work.

THE END

INDEX

THE SOCIETY OF THE INNER LIGHT

The Society of the Inner Light is a Society for the study of Occultism, Mysticism, and Esoteric Psychology and the development of their practice.

Its aims are Christian and its methods are Western.

Students who, after due inquiry, desire to pursue their studies further, may take the Correspondence Course. Their training will be in the theory of Esoteric Science, and they will be given the discipling which prepares for its practice.

For further details apply for a copy of the WORK & AIMS of the Society from:

> The Secretariat
> The Society of the Inner Light
> 38 Steele's Road
> London NW3 4RG
> England

THE INNER LIGHT JOURNAL, a quarterly magazine, founded by Dion Fortune, is devoted to the study of Mysticism, Esoteric Christianity, Occult Science and the Psychology of Superconsciousness. Inquire with the Society at the address above for subscription rates.

Dion Fortune (1891–1946), founder of The
Society of Inner the Light, is recognized as one
of the most luminous and significant figures of
20th-century esoteric thought. A prolific writer,
pioneer psychologist, and powerful psychic,
she dedicated her life to the revival of the
Mystery Tradition of the West. She left behind
a solidly established system of teaching and a
school of initiation based on her knowledge of
many systems, ancient and modern. Her books
were published before World War II, and have
been continuously in demand since that time.